REVELATION

WESLEY BIBLE STUDIES

wphonline.com

Copyright © 2014 by Wesleyan Publishing House
Published by Wesleyan Publishing House
Indianapolis, Indiana 46250
Printed in the United States of America
ISBN: 978-0-89827-878-1
ISBN (e-book): 978-0-89827-879-8

CONTENTS

Introduction   5

1. The Glory of the Eternal Christ
   Revelation 1:1–3, 9–20   7

2. The Presence of Christ in His Church
   Revelation 2:8–29   16

3. What Does Your Church Need?
   Revelation 3:1–22   26

4. A Glimpse of Heaven
   Revelation 4–5   36

5. The Beginning of the End
   Revelation 6:1–17   45

6. The Ultimate Victory Celebration
   Revelation 7:9–17   55

7. Christ Wins; Satan Loses
   Revelation 11:15–19; 12:7–12   64

8. A Heavenly Perspective on Earth
   Revelation 13:1–18   73

9. The Redeemed Follow the Lamb
   Revelation 14:1–13   81

10. Power, Greed, and Faith
    Revelation 17:1–18   90

11. Celebrate the Lamb
    Revelation 19:1–10   99

12. A New Heaven and a New Earth
    Revelation 21:1–7, 22–27   108

13. Come, Lord Jesus
    Revelation 22:1–6, 12–21   117

Words from Wesley Works Cited   126

INTRODUCTION

Jesus Wins!

Several approaches to the book of Revelation are popular today. Some Christians read the Apocalypse with a newspaper in hand, plotting the connections and building theories of the end times. Others approach John's vision with a heart of skepticism, believing it constitutes nothing more than a science fiction short story. Others avoid the book altogether, too confused by the symbols John used or too frightened by his imagery. But when we put down the newspaper, temper our skepticism, or overcome our fears, we find here the beautiful culmination of the story of salvation that began in Genesis.

This climactic "rest of the story" is told with amazing—and bewildering—color and imagery, but a single theme breaks through to give clarity and peace: Jesus, the Lamb of God, overcomes evil and welcomes His children into His kingdom.

Jesus wins!

He defeats the Devil and his army to set the world back in order. In each of these studies, we will follow this theme, this Lamb, and trace the story of the salvation of humankind.

You might wonder why such a mysterious book was chosen to close the canon of Scripture and proclaim God's ultimate victory. Here are three discoveries you will make that will greatly enhance your understanding and love for this prophetic book.

REVELATION LOOKS BACK AS MUCH AS FORWARD

If, while reading Revelation, you discover that some of its references are strangely familiar, don't be alarmed. Revelation contains more than three hundred allusions to the Old Testament. Many were meant to clue us in to the fact that the events described are the fulfillment of past prophecies. In the very first study, Jesus described himself as the Alpha and the Omega. With this phrase Jesus connects the dots of human history. He stood at the very beginning of time, He is now, and He will be in the future.

JESUS IS THE CONQUERING LAMB

While the opening visions of Jesus with blazing eyes and bronze feet are startling, the most powerful image is of Jesus as the slain lamb. This picture poetically brings together two seeming opposites: power and humility. Jesus isn't a brash dictator who takes His victory by force; instead He displays His force through sacrifice and deep love.

JESUS IS COMING AGAIN

Revelation issues a strong appeal for the church of Jesus Christ to be ready for Christ's return. While it is true that He will return, it is also true that the Holy Spirit is now present, working in our midst. The Spirit enlivens the church to do the work Jesus has called us to. Ours is not a distant god. He is here now, and He is coming again.

Conflicting ideas and controversial theories about the events surrounding the end of time have caused many readers to flee from the Revelation in glassy-eyed confusion. That need not be! Through this rich, mysterious writing, we gain confidence of what is (the gospel that we now proclaim) and what will be (the glorious return of our Lord and Christ). Here is the only book of the Bible that comes with a blessing for those who read it.

Dig in, and discover this blessing for yourself!

1

THE GLORY OF THE ETERNAL CHRIST

Revelation 1:1–3, 9–20

God has a plan for the future, and He is ready to reveal it.

People love to argue about meaningless details. That was true of the Pharisees and Sadducees, who peppered Jesus with trick questions. It was true of early Christians, whom Paul warned to avoid "godless myths and old wives' tales" (1 Tim. 4:7). And it is often true of believers today.

This study will help you get past relatively unimportant details, such as the exact date and time of Christ's return, and focus on the big picture—God's ultimate plan to redeem humankind. Jesus is the central figure in this plan, and the awesome description of Him in these verses reassures all believers that He already won the ultimate victory.

COMMENTARY

Revelation is intriguing, yet perplexing. Written in the form of an epistle, it was intended for a specific audience, addressing specific concerns and needs. Many people avoid reading it due to the generous use of symbols and metaphors. However, it is the only book of the Bible accompanied by a promise of blessing for its readers.

Revelation is best described as "apocalyptic literature." (The word *apocalypse* means "revelation" or "unveiling.") This style of writing was popular from 200 B.C. to A.D. 100. The writer often took the reader on a journey outside reality to deal with issues too personal and tender to deal with directly. The writer unveiled difficult truths for the reader, assigning commonly known characters, places, and events to symbolic or imaginary creatures and places. In doing so, the writer recorded events from the perspective of the hidden reality not seen in the history written by the rich and powerful.

Revelation is prophetic. The apocalyptic writers wrote in the tradition of the prophets. They borrowed from the prophets, but they held to a view that favored a more dramatic end of the world. Where the prophets predicted judgment, the apocalyptic writers dramatized it. They used graphic language and frightening creatures and symbols to foretell what was to come.

Revelation conveys the ongoing battle between good and evil. Apocalyptic writers incorporated angels and demons as important characters in the drama, with angels often serving as tour guides and interpreters. The attitude of the apocalyptic writers was generally pessimistic.

The book of Revelation is generally interpreted through one of four viewpoints: the futurist view, the historicist view, the idealist view, and the preterist view. All four divide the book between the third and fourth chapters as differentiating between what is and what is to come. The futurist view is the most well-known position. This position asserts that the events depicted after chapter 3 are yet to be fulfilled. The historicist approach views the events of Revelation as an overarching course of history from the time of the apostles to the end of the world. Fulfillment has been going on for two thousand years and continues now. This view is the historic Protestant interpretation. The idealist position interprets the book as a great drama displaying transcendent spiritual realities, such as the many conflicts between good and evil, rather than identifying specific fulfillments of the events, visions, and symbols. The preterist perspective places fulfillment soon after it was written, in the first century — in ancient history from our vantage point, but still future to the author. Some preterists believe the final chapters depict the coming of Christ, while others believe the entire book is complete in fulfillment.

The Book Introduced by John (Rev. 1:1–3)

The opening sentence states the book's purpose and produces controversy as to its exact meaning: Does the phrase **the revelation from Jesus Christ** (v. 1) denote Jesus as the revealer or the revealed? Either interpretation is supported by the language. The stated purpose of the book is **to show his servants what must soon take place** (v. 1). Ultimately, Jesus is both the revealer and the revealed. What must take place involves a revelation of Jesus. The events described in Revelation cannot be separated from Jesus. He actively accompanies the action, often instituting it. The message and events give us a greater understanding of Jesus, and a glimpse into His majesty, glory, and authority.

WORDS FROM WESLEY
Revelation 1:1

It is a great thing to be a servant of Jesus Christ. This book is dedicated particularly to the servants of Christ in the seven churches in Asia: but not exclusive of all His other servants, in all nations and ages. It is one single revelation, and yet sufficient for them all, from the time it was written to the end of the world. Serve thou the Lord Jesus Christ in truth. So shalt thou learn His secret in this book. Yea, and thou shalt feel in thy heart, whether this book be divine or not. *The things which must shortly come to pass*—The things contained in this prophecy did begin to be accomplished shortly after it was given; and the whole might be said to come to pass shortly, in the same sense as St. Peter says the end of all things is at hand; and our Lord himself, Behold, I come quickly. There is in this book a rich treasure of all the doctrines pertaining to faith and holiness. But these are also delivered in other parts of holy writ; so that the revelation need not to have been given for the sake of these. The peculiar design of this is, to show the things which must come to pass. And this we are especially to have before our eyes, whenever we read or hear it. (ENNT)

The message came to John by means of an angel. John, an eyewitness of the life of Jesus, was now a witness of all the angel showed him, containing both **the word of God and the testimony of Jesus** (v. 2). Both are ways of describing the gospel.

Again, this is the only biblical book accompanied by the promise of a blessing, the first of seven beatitudes found in Revelation. This blessing is twofold, involving both the reader and the one who hears and obeys it. Because the book of Revelation was originally a letter, not every individual could read it for him- or herself. Hence the differentiation between the reader, who would read the letter in the public assembly, and those who would hear the reading. The blessing further extends to those who would read, hear, and obey these words down through history. The fact that an admonition to obedience accompanies the blessing indicates moral instruction as well as prediction. This response is required **because the time is near** (v. 3), indicating an urgency to reading, hearing, and responding to the message.

WORDS FROM WESLEY

Revelation 1:3

Happy is he that readeth, and they that hear the words of this prophecy—Some have miserably handled this book. Hence others are afraid to touch it. And while they desire to know all things else, reject only the knowledge of those which God hath shown. They inquire after any thing rather than this; as if it were written, happy is he that doth *not* read this prophecy. Nay, but *happy is he that readeth, and they that hear* and keep the words thereof: especially at this time, when so considerable a part of them is on the point of being fulfilled. . . . Our Lord foretold many things before His passion; but not all things: for it was not yet seasonable. Many things, likewise, His Spirit foretold in the writings of the apostles, so far as the necessities of those times required; now He comprises them all in one short book: therein presupposing all the other prophecies, and, at the same time, explaining, continuing, and perfecting them in one thread. (ENNT)

The Son of Man Described by John (Rev. 1:9–16)

Immediately following a greeting and doxology directed to the recipients, John launched into his first vision. He began by establishing the context, indentifying with his readers as **brother and companion** (v. 9). The term **brother** was common for those in the faith, denoting the familial relationship through Christ. The term **companion** brings to mind the relationship of fellow travelers on this journey of faith, enduring common hardships. Their brotherhood and companionship was tied by **suffering and kingdom and patient endurance** (v. 9).

Suffering refers to the consequences of living as a believer in Jesus. Regardless of the date for the writing of Revelation, A.D. 67 or 95, intense persecution was upon the church. Christians were being imprisoned or put to death—many in the coliseum as part of Rome's public entertainment.

Kingdom refers to the already-established reign of Jesus through His atoning work. This includes the messianic blessedness promised to those who follow Him. John reminded his readers of Jesus' promise that they would be blessed because of their persecution. Additionally, he called them to a life of hope, looking to the future when Jesus would return.

Patient endurance refers to the attitude John called his readers to reflect. All through Revelation he assured them that this present suffering was only for a while and offered hope that those who endured would receive a great reward.

John began writing Revelation **on the island of Patmos** (v. 9) **on the Lord's Day** (v. 10). Church tradition has established that John was exiled there by the Roman government, which often banished those they perceived as a threat to the order and goodwill of the empire. **The Lord's Day** is generally accepted as the first day of the week, which had become the day of celebration and worship for the Christian church.

WORDS FROM WESLEY

Revelation 1:9

This book peculiarly belongs to those who are under the cross. It was given to a banished man: and men in affliction understand and relish it most. Accordingly it was little esteemed by the Asiatic church, after the time of Constantine; but highly valued by all the African churches, as it has been since by all the persecuted children of God. (ENNT)

In the tradition of Ezekiel and Isaiah, John received his call to ministry accompanied by a vision of Jesus. He wrote, **I heard behind me a loud voice like a trumpet** (v. 10). The voice instructed him: **"Write on a scroll what you see and send it to the seven churches: to Ephesus, Smyrna, Pergamum, Thyatira, Sardis, Philadelphia and Laodicea"** (v. 11). These churches were likely chosen because they probably comprised the major postal centers of Asia. The number seven has significance, indicating completeness, which may translate to the message being for all churches of all time, not just seven historical churches of Asia.

John then arrived at the actual vision: **I turned around to see the voice that was speaking to me** (v. 12). We rarely think of seeing a voice. This sentence makes us think that the voice was so awesome John expected it to be part of a great scene. Like a mighty waterfall, the sound elicits the expectation of a grand visual display. John was greeted with just such a scene. **And when I turned I saw seven golden lampstands** (v. 12). John turned to see the voice, but the first thing he saw was the lampstands. These stands each held an oil lamp on top. We are not given any indication as to their arrangement, but **among the lampstands was someone "like a son of man"** (v. 13). Again, details are left to our imagination; John did not specify how the person was among the lampstands. His presence was significant, however, as we will see later.

By using the term **son of man**, John guided his audience toward thinking of a passage common to them, Daniel 7. His use of the phrase was no accident; undoubtedly he hoped to stimulate his audience to reflect on the similarities. This term was the most common description used by Jesus for himself. In this phrase, John brilliantly introduced Jesus as the character he envisioned and established Jesus' divinity by linking the vision to the Daniel passage.

The one **"like a son of man"** was **dressed in a robe reaching down to his feet** (Rev. 1:13). This indicates a priestly robe, establishing one of the roles of Jesus. A further role—that of king—is defined by the description of **a golden sash around his chest** (v. 13). The description of His head and hair match those given in Daniel. However, in Daniel the blazing fire projects from His throne, and in Revelation **his eyes were like blazing fire** (1:14). Below His robe could be seen His feet **like bronze glowing in a furnace** (v. 15). The voice that originally captured John's attention is again described as **the sound of rushing waters** (v. 15), bringing to mind a great waterfall thundering over the rocks.

The number seven surfaces again as John described the stars held in Jesus' right hand. The word of God is portrayed as **a sharp double-edged sword** (v. 16) coming out of His mouth. **His face was like the sun shining in all its brilliance** (v. 16). There is no doubt that this image took John back to a moment on the top of a mountain where he had seen Jesus in all His glory.

Instructions Recorded by John (Rev. 1:17–20)

John responded to this vision in a manner typical to the human encountering the divine. He **fell at his feet as though dead** (v. 17). Jesus reached out His hand to assure John that all was well. If any doubt was left regarding His identity, it was now removed with the words that followed. Jesus described himself with phrases unique to His character and affirming of His divinity. This assurance was followed by instructions reiterating the purpose stated in verse 1.

Jesus gave John an explanation of the stars in His hand and the lampstands surrounding Him. Jesus amid the churches, represented by the lampstands, is an assuring and appropriate picture. It is in the gathered church that the presence of Jesus is found.

As John launched into this great work of the Revelation of Jesus Christ, it is appropriate that he would begin with a picture of Jesus. He established the presence of Jesus in His church and in His specific churches. He established the divinity of Jesus and His role as prophet, priest, and king. Those first hearing this message during intense persecution would receive tremendous hope that they had not been forgotten by Jesus. Though He ascended, He is still present with them. We also rejoice in this great promise.

WORDS FROM WESLEY

Revelation 1:17

And I fell at his feet as dead—Human nature not being able to sustain so glorious an appearance. Thus was he prepared (like Daniel of old whom he particularly resembles) for receiving so weighty a prophecy. A great sinking of nature usually precedes a large communication of heavenly things. St. John, before our Lord suffered, was so intimate with Him, as to lean on His breast, to lie in His bosom. Yet now, near seventy years after, the aged apostle is by one glance struck to the ground. What a glory must this be! Ye sinners, be afraid. Cleanse your hands. Purify your hearts. Ye saints, be humble. Prepare. Rejoice. But rejoice unto Him with reverence. An increase of reverence towards this awful majesty can be no prejudice to your faith. Let all petulancy, with all vain curiosity, be far away, while you are thinking or reading of these things. (ENNT)

DISCUSSION

Discuss why you think people are often more interested in the events of Revelation than *the* revelation.

1. Why is it significant that John described the book as the "revelation of Jesus Christ" rather than the revelation of things to come?

2. What things do you believe John wanted the readers to "take to heart"?

3. How does the description of the heavenly Jesus in verses 12–15 compare to the descriptions of Jesus found in the Gospels?

4. What are your feelings toward this revelation of Jesus?

5. How does Jesus' description of himself in verse 18 compare to John's in Revelation 14:5–11; 16:28; 17:1–5?

6. Although Jesus' appearance is understandably frightening, why would He say, "Do not be afraid"?

7. In what ways does Jesus comfort our fears about life and death?

8. The world is fascinated with popular books and theories about the end times. Why do you think Revelation is addressed to the church and not to the world?

PRAYER

O Christ our Lord and King, we fall before You in total submission in the face of Your glory, majesty, and holiness. Purify our minds and strengthen our faith, so that we will become like You in this world.

2

THE PRESENCE OF CHRIST IN HIS CHURCH

Revelation 2:8–29

Jesus communicates to His church with compassion.

Do you like to receive mail? Some people eagerly await the daily delivery from the post office or check their e-mail dozens of times each day. It's always nice to get a letter from a friend or some news about an important event. Yet sometimes the mail brings bad news. Bills, tax notices, court judgments are all delivered by the same letter carrier who brings birthday cards and sweepstakes offerings. Our response to the mail may depend on whether it includes a check or a challenge.

What if the letter was sent by Jesus himself and described in detail your spiritual status, offering both encouragement and correction? This study describes that very scenario. Early in the history of the church, Jesus personally addressed seven congregations living in the region we call Asia Minor. Some churches were known for their faithfulness, others were chided for being lazy, and all were warned of coming challenges. The message to each? Pay attention to your spiritual condition and be faithful.

The warnings to these churches were not meant for them alone but for all Christians who would follow. This study will serve as our own "letter" from Jesus, reminding today's church that the Lord knows when to commend and when to correct, and that we must persevere to the end.

COMMENTARY

Revelation 1:20 is a key to unlocking 2:1: "These are the words of him who holds the seven stars in his right hand and walks among the seven golden lampstands." The stars are the angels of the churches, and the lampstands are the churches. Christ's presence is imminent in the church. He holds it and walks among it. In the messages to the seven churches, Christ showed that He knew them and was with them.

WORDS FROM WESLEY
Revelation 2:1

Write—So Christ dictated to him every word. *These things saith he who holdeth the seven stars in his right hand*—Such is His mighty power! Such His favour to them, and care over them, that they may indeed shine as stars, both by purity of doctrine and holiness of life! *Who walketh*—According to His promise, *I am with you always, even to the end of the world: in the midst of the golden candlesticks*—Beholding all their works and thoughts, and ready to *remove the candlestick out of its place*—If any being warned, will not repent. Perhaps here is likewise an allusion to the office of the priests in dressing the lamps, which was to keep them always burning before the Lord. (ENNT)

In each of the letters to the seven churches the angel of the church is specifically addressed (see Rev. 2:1, 8, 12, 18). But what is the meaning of the "angel of a church"? Eastern Orthodox Churches believe when a church building is dedicated, God assigns it a guardian angel. Since the fall of Communism, the Russian Orthodox Church has tried to identify these "angel-ed" churches for restoration.

The term for *angel* in the Greek text means "messenger" and could be translated that way. The apostle John used the term as many as fifty times in Revelation, and the meaning is most often a heavenly messenger. The Greek text in chapters 1–3 could be translated *messengers* "of the seven churches." Or individually "To the *messenger* of the church in . . ." So it may mean the pastor of the church.

Each of the first four letters to the churches follows a similar pattern:

- The address: "To the angel of the church in . . . write" (2:1, 8, 12, 18). Note that *church* is singular to a specific church.
- An "I know" statement (2:2, 9, 13, 19) in which Christ relates a fact or two about the particular church.
- An encouraging word and a corrective word.
- A general command to the churches (note the plural in 2:7, 11, 17, 29) to overcome.
- A promise for the churches—both a specific message for overcoming and a general message to overcome.

Smyrna: The Poor Rich Church (Rev. 2:8–11)

Smyrna was a trading center in a beautiful harbor that was easily defended. It has been called the "Crown of Asia" and was one of the earliest Asian cities to align with Rome.

WORDS FROM WESLEY
Revelation 2:8

These things saith the First and the Last, who was dead and is alive—How directly does this description tend to confirm Him against the fear of death! ver. 10, 11. Even with the comfort wherewith St. John himself was comforted ch. 1:17, 18 shall the angel of this church be comforted. (ENNT)

The description of Jesus as **the First and the Last** (v. 8) mirrors Isaiah 44:6: "This is what the LORD says—Israel's King and

Redeemer, the LORD Almighty: I am the first and I am the last; apart from me there is no God." It is a reference to Christ's divine nature. The second part of Revelation 2:8 is a description of Christ's death and resurrection: **who died and came to life again**. These two primary theological statements—that Christ is God and that He died and rose again—were the doctrines most probably attacked by the enemies of the church in Smyrna.

Verse 9 gives two things Christ knew about this church. First, **I know your afflictions**. The Greek root for **affliction** means pressure. This church was continually under scrutiny and accusation by the Jews of the city. Jesus called them the **synagogue of Satan** (v. 9). This lead to the admonition, **Do not be afraid of what you are about to suffer** (v. 10). In a prophetic word of knowledge John warned that pressure will culminate in actual suffering, **even to the point of death**. The second thing Christ knew about this church was about their **poverty—yet** they were **rich** (v. 9). Christians were often the lower classes or slaves in society. Their houses and businesses were targeted for looting by mobs. But Christ knew they were rich in Him. This can be contrasted to the church of Laodicea (3:17), which claimed to be rich but was poor.

WORDS FROM WESLEY
Revelation 2:9

I know thy affliction and poverty—A poor prerogative in the eyes of the world! The angel at Philadelphia likewise had in their sight but a *little strength*. And yet these two were the most honourable of all in the eyes of the Lord. *But thou art rich*—In faith and love, of more value than all the kingdoms of the earth. *Who say they are Jews*—God's own people, *and are not*—They are not Jews inwardly, not circumcised in heart: *But a synagogue of Satan*—Who, like them, was a liar and a murderer, from the beginning. (ENNT)

Unlike most of the other letters to the churches, there is no corrective statement to the church of Smyrna. There is, however, the promise given by the **Spirit . . . to the churches. He who overcomes will not be hurt at all by the second death** (2:11). When we understand that physical life is of less importance than the life to come, values reverse. Giving up what is of least value for that of greatest value is a good trade. Experiencing physical death in exchange for escaping the second death is wise.

Pergamum: Living in Satan's Realm (Rev. 2:12–17)

Situated north of Smyrna and fifteen miles inland, Pergamum's power laid in its connection with Rome. The description of Christ as **him who has the sharp, double-edged sword** (v. 12) may be a reference to this power. Roman officials were divided into two classes: those with the sword and those without. A Roman official with the sword had the power of life or death. John reminded the church of Pergamum that Christ is the one with the ultimate power.

Pergamum was surrounded by hilltop temples to pagan gods, but people subjugated by Rome were required to come once a year to burn incense before a magistrate (with the sword) and to declare, "Caesar is Lord." A certificate was issued and the individual could then worship any god he or she liked. Those who refused to give Caesar ultimate worship were declared enemies of Rome and sentenced to death. Christ says, **I know where you live—where Satan has his throne. Yet you remain true to my name. You did not renounce your faith in me** (v. 13). Jesus knew; He saw; He understood. He commended those who lived their faith in a sinful world. **Antipas, my faithful witness, who was put to death** (v. 13) was especially commended. It is not that the Lord expects His servants to seek out confrontation with Satan's kingdom, but when we are forced to take a stand, then we must say boldly, "Jesus is Lord," not Caesar. Antipas was our hero of faith.

The false teaching of **Balaam** was compromised with the world **to entice the Israelites to sin by eating food sacrificed to idols and by committing sexual immorality** (v. 14). The first lie of the Devil was "You will not surely die" (Gen. 3:4); this is a lie he is still declaring through the Balaams in the church. God says **remain true to my name** (Rev. 2:13).

The one who overcomes will be given **some of the hidden manna** and **a white stone with a new name written on it** (v. 17). While there are probably first-century cultural implications to each of these descriptions, the meaning is simple: The promise is God's care and a new identity, a new creation under new management. Those who overcome live on a different level.

WORDS FROM WESLEY
Revelation 2:17

To him that overcometh—And eateth not of those sacrifices; *will I give of the hidden manna*—Described John 6. The new name answers to this; it is now *hid with Christ in God.* The Jewish manna was kept in the ancient ark of the covenant. The heavenly ark of the covenant appears under the trumpet of the seventh angel, ch. 11:19 where also *the hidden manna* is mentioned again. It seems properly to mean, the full, glorious, everlasting fruition of God. *And I will give him a white stone*—The ancients, on many occasions, gave their votes on judgment by small stones: by black they condemned; by white ones they acquitted. Sometimes also they wrote on small, smooth stones. Here may be an allusion to both. *And a new name*—So Jacob, after his victory, gained the new name of Israel. Wouldst thou know what thy *new name* will be: the way to this is plain; *overcome.* Till then all thy inquiries are vain. Thou wilt then read it on the *white stone.* (ENNT)

Thyatira: Compromised Worship (Rev. 2:18–29)

Thyatira was a trade city on the road to Pergamum. Little is known about the city except it appears to have had many trade guilds, and scholars speculate that these trade unions were a part of the problem in the church.

Christ is identified as **the Son of God, whose eyes are like a blazing fire and whose feet are like burnished bronze** (v. 18; compare 1:14–16). The title **Son of God** is the one that brought condemnation by the Sanhedrin (see Matt. 26:63–68). This title set Jesus against Jewish leadership; it was not politically correct. The picture is of firm stance and steel in the eye over an issue that cannot be compromised.

Here is what the Son of God knew about the church in Thyatira: Their actions and their faith were solid and growing. **I know your deeds, your love and faith, your service and perseverance, and that you are now doing more than you did at first** (Rev. 2:19). This is a picture of a healthy church. The word for **love** here is *agape* in the Greek, a deep-seated godly love that outflows in deeds and service. The congregation at Thyatira was experiencing a growing faith and a steadfast stance and advance in the face of opposition.

WORDS FROM WESLEY
Revelation 2:24

But I say to you, who *do not hold this doctrine*—Of Jezebel; *who have not known the depths of Satan*—O happy ignorance! *as they speak*—That were continually boasting of the *deep things* which they taught. Our Lord owns they were *deep*, even deep as hell; for they were the very depths of Satan. Were these the same of which Martin Luther speaks? 'Tis well if there are not some of his countrymen, now in England, who know them too well; *I will lay upon you no other burden*—Than that you have already suffered from Jezebel and her adherents. (ENNT)

There was a problem, though: **You tolerate that woman Jezebel, who calls herself a prophetess** (v. 20). Here was a church that outwardly had everything going for it. It was growing in faith and deed. There was real love. But just under the surface was a cancer that probably took this church under. It did not last into the second century.

Jezebel was, of course, the Phoenician wife of Ahab (see 1 Kings 18:4). The problem Jezebel had with the religion of Israel was that it was intolerant of Baal worship. She wanted them to compromise just a little, live and let live; but they would not. In Thyatira there were two areas of contention: **sexual immorality and the eating of food sacrificed to idols** (Rev. 2:20). These are the things this prophetess was **teaching**. We can only speculate on what was happening. It may be that to work in Thyatira it was necessary to belong to a union that would have a patron god. Union meetings would be a feast dedicated to a particular god. Missing the union meeting could put you out of work. What was the Christian to do? In keeping with the Old Testament, John called it sexual immorality and **adultery** (v. 22; compare Ex. 34:15–16; Deut. 31:15; Hos. 5:4).

WORDS FROM WESLEY

Revelation 2:28

I will give him the morning-star — Thou, O Jesus, art the morning-star. O give thyself to me! Then will I desire no sun, only thee, who art the sun also. He whom this star enlightens, has always morning and no evening. The duties and promises here answer each other. The valiant conqueror has power over the stubborn nations. And he that, after having conquered his enemies, keeps the words of Christ to the end, shall *have the morning-star* — an unspeakable brightness and peaceful dominion in him. (ENNT)

The admonition to overcome has a different emphasis here. **Hold on to what you have until I come. To him who overcomes and does my will to the end, I will give authority over**

the nations (Rev. 2:25–26). Overcoming must last to the final breath. The idea that if you once had faith you cannot fall is the fallacious teaching of this prophetess. The message that needs to be heard by the churches is the necessity of overcoming.

The **morning star** is a symbol of tranquility. The picture in verse 28 is early morning when there is light enough to see but not enough to blot out that one morning star. When the wind is calm and sound travels long distances, the dew is still on the grass, just as the birds begin to put their heads up to sing. That tranquil moment of peace is the promise for the one who overcomes. **I will also give him the morning star** (v. 28).

DISCUSSION

Jesus is alive and active in the church of Christ today. Let us never forget that.

1. What do you think is meant by Jesus holding the church in His hands? Does He do that today?

2. What do you think is meant by Jesus walking among the churches? Does He do that today?

3. How would you describe the church in Smyrna?

4. How is it possible for a church to be in poverty and yet be rich?

5. What comfort in the church's persecution did Jesus offer?

6. Notice that Jesus used facets of His earlier description to address the individual churches. Why do you think He used the "sharp, double-edged sword" image for the church in Pergamum?

7. What issues in Pergamum are churches facing today?

8. What one-word command is given to the church in Pergamum? How it that applicable to the church today?

9. Jesus described an "intolerable" situation in Thyatira. In what ways does the church today tolerate sin?

PRAYER

Lord, give us the wisdom and discipline to live a life rich in spiritual treasure. Help us to remain faithful and fruitful in the face of wickedness as we grow in love for each other and You.

3

WHAT DOES YOUR CHURCH NEED?

Revelation 3:1–22

Christ will speak to churches that are willing to listen.

Sometimes God seems to give us exactly what we want at that moment. At other times, He seems to ignore what we have in mind for ourselves and give us what we truly need. As we all know, wants and needs are two separate things. This is true for individual believers and for congregations as well.

Each of the churches mentioned in Revelation 3 had a particular need. That need was local, meaning it had to do with the particular circumstances of believers living in that time and place. In each case, Jesus pointed out the need in terms that may have been surprising—even uncomfortable—to His hearers. Like children, these congregations did not necessarily know what was best for them until Jesus identified it.

COMMENTARY

As mentioned in the previous study, all of the letters in Revelation 2–3 follow a similar pattern:

- A description of the divine author.
- Comments on the present condition of each church, both negative and positive.
- Warnings and instructions for each church.
- A promise to its faithful members.
- A closing invitation to hear what the Spirit has spoken.

Jesus' Letter to Sardis (Rev. 3:1–6)

The letter to Sardis opens by describing Jesus as the one **who holds the seven spirits of God and the seven stars** (v. 1). The first phrase appears in 1:4 and may refer to Isaiah 11:2 (that mentions seven spheres of the Holy Spirit's ministry). The second phrase refers to the seven churches to whom Jesus, through John, was writing. Each of these, including Sardis, belongs to God and is figuratively held in His hand.

Jesus offered several comments on the present state of the church at Sardis. **I know your deeds; you have a reputation of being alive, but you are dead** (Rev. 3:1). **I have not found your deeds complete in the sight of my God** (v. 2). **Yet you have a few people in Sardis who have not soiled their clothes** (v. 4). Jesus saw little in this church to criticize, for this church had not fallen into overwhelming sin or heresy (as others among the six churches had). But neither was there much to praise. The church at Sardis contained no life. Perhaps its people lacked energy to move either backward or forward. Lethargy may have kept them on the right path, but they seemed stuck. The church was not growing; its few people muddled along harmlessly.

What would Jesus say to such a church? **Wake up!** (v. 2). If the church in Sardis became more lively, what would it look like? Stronger. A healthier memory. Obedient. Repentant. These words present a picture of church health.

Remember . . . what you have received and heard (v. 3). The Christians of Sardis had heard of Jesus, the Life, the One who had conquered death (both the death of individuals and the sad state of churches that were barely surviving). These people had not only heard the message of Jesus, but the risen Lord had come to live in their community. Jesus asked if the church was slipping toward death by forgetting its source of life.

WORDS FROM WESLEY

Revelation 3:3

Remember how—Humbly, zealously, seriously, thou didst receive the grace of God once, *and hear*—His word; *and hold fast*—The grace thou hast received; *and repent*—According to the word thou hast heard. (ENNT)

Strengthen what remains and is about to die (v. 2). Could the Sardis church renew itself? No, but it could do its part to reestablish connection with the source of life and strength.

Repent (v. 3). The Christians at Sardis needed to recognize that God remained as faithful as ever; if their close relationship with God had dwindled, God had not moved away. Jesus offered these believers a chance to return to Him, to offer Him the same loyalty they did when He first rescued them (from either legalism or paganism).

Obey (v. 3). Jesus wanted to give the Christians at Sardis the strength they needed to move forward, to walk with Him in obedience that would bring ongoing transformation to them and their community.

If the church in Sardis refused these instructions, if they continued toward the sleep of spiritual death, Jesus would appear among them (v. 4), and not to pass out awards. Did Jesus here refer to His second coming, to be seen by all the world? Probably not. As Christians today pray for the Spirit of Christ to appear among them in blessing, so Christ can arrive at churches with judgment, to close the doors of churches that are moving toward death by merely going through the motions.

For those in Sardis who actively sought to live for Jesus, what promises did He offer? **They will walk with me, dressed in white, for they are worthy. He who overcomes will, like them, be dressed in white. I will never blot out his name from the book**

of life, but will acknowledge his name before my Father and his angels (vv. 4–5). In contrast to dying people who anticipate nothing but being buried in a hole, those who are truly alive can walk with Jesus. Twenty-first-century Christians use this phrase so often we forget its meaning. Walking involves movement, progress.

Not only did Jesus contrast the positions of those who are awake and asleep, moving and comatose, but He pointed out a difference in their clothing. Ancient Christians (and many modern believers) wore white robes at the time of their baptism. This color represents spiritual and moral purity God restored to them. Had the Christians of Sardis moved into gross sin that had **soiled their clothes** (v. 4)? Not that Jesus mentioned. But neither had they maintained a vital relationship with Jesus that would have kept their garments clean. To those who did walk with Christ, He promised ongoing cleanliness, in this life and the next.

This passage includes John's first mention of the Book of Life. (See also 13:8; 17:8; 20:12, 15; 21:27.) The Bible's first reference to a divine record book came in a conversation Moses had with the Father at the base of Mount Sinai (Ex. 32:32–33). The inclusion or exclusion of an individual's name from God's book indicates the existence of his or her living relationship with God. Jesus promises the church He will acknowledge the names of the faithful before His Father (Rev. 3:5). This promise parallels words Matthew recorded (Matt. 10:32–33).

Jesus' Letter to Philadelphia (Rev. 3:7–13)

To this church, Jesus introduced himself as the One **who is holy and true, who holds the key of David** (v. 7). (These introductory words are likely interchangeable. That is, in the seven letters, Jesus gave seven descriptions of himself, but may not have had special reason for tying any introduction to the content of each letter.) Holiness implies both God's purity and His transcendence. When you hear Jesus portray himself as **true**, hear Him saying not so much that He speaks the truth (although that is an accurate statement), but that He is faithful, like a true friend. **The key of David**? Jesus presented himself as the fulfillment of Old Testament messianic prophecies, the One whom King David foreshadowed. But Jesus was not only King of the Jews, for He rules the universe. With His power, represented by a key, He rules over all, and can overrule anyone or anything that stands in His way.

WORDS FROM WESLEY

Revelation 3:7

The Holy One, the True One—Two great and glorious names. *He that hath the key of David*—A master of a family, or a prince, has one or more keys wherewith he can open and shut all the doors of his house or palace. So had David a key (a token of right and sovereignty), which was afterward adjudged to Eliakim, Isaiah 22:22. Much more has Christ the Son of David, the key of the sipirtual city of David, the New Jerusalem: the supreme right, power, and authority, as in His own house. He openeth this to all that overcome, *and none shutteth*—He shutteth it against all the fearful; *and none openeth*—Likewise, when He openeth a door on earth for His work or His servants, none can shut; and when He shutteth against whatever would hurt or defile, none can open. (ENNT)

What did Christ know of this church's circumstances? **I know that you have little strength, yet you have kept my word and have not denied my name** (v. 8). God relishes His ability to use unexpected people. David, whom Jesus had just mentioned, was the runt of his family, yet became Israel's greatest Old Testament king. As God could use little David, so He could use even a weak church devoted to Christ's commands, despite opposition (3:10; compare 2 Cor. 12:9). For this church that was eager to move out for Jesus (compare sedentary Sardis), God delighted in opening a door of ministry.

Opposition? **The synagogue of Satan** (people)**, who claim to be Jews though they are not, but are liars** (Rev. 3:9). As both Jesus and the apostle Paul had faced Jews who tried to destroy them and their ministries, so Christians of Lydia (Philadelphia was a city in Lydia) still faced this danger. Those Jews who truly worshiped God had recognized Jesus as God's Son. (Compare the Berean Jews of Acts 17:11–12.) Those who worshiped their own Jewish system could claim a position in God's favor, but their denial of the true God who had come among them showed their claims to be no more than lies. The open door of ministry Jesus gave the Philadelphian church would include a fruitful ministry among the Jews, some of whom would become servants of the church and its Lord (see Rev. 3:9).

Would faithfulness among believers in Philadelphia protect them from all pain? No, they would, with God's help, be able to survive, endure, even thrive during the persecution that would arise (v. 10). Would this time of trial be one that immediately preceded Jesus' return? The opening words of verse 11 — **I am coming soon** — would lead one to answer affirmatively. It might be wiser, however, for us to interpret these words as indicating God's people had moved into the last times, the last times of which Christians have been a part for two thousand years.

Instructions for the Philadelphians? **Hold on** (v. 11). This church did not need to wake up, to start doing anything new. In their weakness, however, Jesus instructed them not to give up, but to keep depending on Him for strength for their tasks. Jesus did not intend **Hold on** as a pessimistic invitation to hide from the church's enemies, but as a call to move out in love and power, seeking to bring resistant ones to Jesus.

Again, Jesus followed His instructions with guarantees: **No one will** be able to **take your crown. . . . I will make** you **a pillar** in the temple of my God. . . . I will write on you the name of my God and His eternal city . . . and I will also write on you my new name (vv. 11–12). Those who overcome, those who remain faithful witnesses of Jesus, may suffer in the short run, but nothing can separate them from the love of God in Christ Jesus their Lord. (See Rom. 8:38–39.)

Jesus gave much praise to the church in Philadelphia. But its members also faced a choice. Would they remain faithful? History shows that they did.

WORDS FROM WESLEY
Revelation 3:15

I know thy works—Thy disposition and behaviour, though thou knowest it not thyself; *that thou art neither cold*—An utter stranger to the things of God, having no care or thought about them; *nor hot*—As boiling water: so ought we to be penetrated and heated by the fire of love. *O that thou wert*—This wish of our Lord plainly implies that He does not work on us irresistibly, as the fire does on the water which it heats; *cold or hot*—Even if thou wert cold, without any thought or profession of religion, there would be more hope of thy recovery. (ENNT)

Jesus' Letter to Laodicea (Rev. 3:14–22)

In introducing himself, Jesus followed the pattern set in His previous letter, highlighting His faithfulness and power.

What characteristics of this church caught Jesus' attention? This church was not dying as Sardis was. This church was not weak as Philadelphia was. No, this church thought it was doing pretty well (v. 17). Perhaps the Christians in Laodicea were energetically running many programs they saw as valuable. This church may have mistaken busyness for faithfulness. Members were doing enough to look respectable but had forgotten one essential factor—to allow Jesus into their fellowship (v. 20).

Had Christians in Laodicea been following Jesus wholeheartedly they would have been fine. Had members of this church been pagan they could have become a target for Christian mission. But, living in a delusion of thinking they were serving God, they found themselves in a no-man's land that Jesus described using an analogy of temperature: **lukewarm** (v. 16).

Although they thought they were doing just fine, Jesus pointed out that the emperor wore no clothes. This church, in all its supposed finery was **naked** (v. 17). If these metaphors weren't enough, Jesus threw in a few more: **wretched, pitiful, poor,** and **blind** (v. 17).

WORDS FROM WESLEY

Revelation 3:18

I counsel thee—Who art *poor, and blind, and naked, to buy of me*—Without money or price, *gold purified in the fire*—True living faith, which is purified in the furnace of affliction; *and white raiment*—True holiness, *and eye-salve*—Spiritual illumination; the unction of the Holy One, which teacheth all things. (ENNT)

Instructions? First, receive the help Jesus offered. Verse 18 lists spiritual solutions for three of the church's metaphorical spiritual problems. In place of poverty, Jesus offered **gold**. For **nakedness, white clothes**. For blindness, **salve**. Second, accept the rebuke and discipline Jesus gave. Third, in response to the rebuke, take concrete steps the metaphors picture: earnestly **repent** (v. 19).

WORDS FROM WESLEY

Revelation 3:20

I stand at the door and knock—Even at this instant; while he is speaking this word; *If any man open*—Willingly receive Me: *I will sup with him*—Refreshing him with My graces and gifts, and delighting myself in what I have given; *and he with we*—In life everlasting. (ENNT)

John called the Christians in Philadelphia to recognize Jesus as **the faithful and true witness** (v. 14). If they did, they would trust Him. In place of seeking their own will, John called them to submit to Him who is **ruler of God's creation** (v. 14). Offering yet another analogical picture, Jesus asked them to open the door of their church to let Him in. (Catch the irony that He who holds the "key of David," who can open doors "no one can shut" [v. 7], stands patiently outside this door, waiting to be invited to enter.)

Promises? The church that welcomes Jesus will see Jesus become an active participant in its fellowship and ministry (v. 20). Those people who actively follow Jesus will become active participants in the fellowship of the Father and Son (v. 21).

The response from the believers in Philadelphia? Verse 22 leaves us uncertain as to their action but communicates that Jesus gave even the lukewarm church a chance to heat up.

DISCUSSION

Reflect on how active you sense Jesus is in your church.

1. How would you describe the church in Sardis? What are the similarities to churches today?

2. The "thief in the night" symbol is used in Matthew 24:36–44. What is the application for today?

3. The church in Philadelphia is described as having "little strength" (Rev. 3:8). What does a church with little strength look like?

4. The church in Laodicea is infamous as the "lukewarm" church? What does a lukewarm church look like?

5. The church in Laodicea also put its trust in its wealth, rather than the riches of Christ? Have you seen modern-day churches fall into that trap? How?

6. Jesus expressed "tough love" to the Laodicea church, yet churches today are often reluctant to exercise discipline within themselves. Why do you think that is?

7. What are ways today that the church can be "wretched, pitiful, poor, blind and naked" (v. 17)?

8. How would you apply the remedy that Jesus names to the modern-day church?

9. We often use verse 20 as an evangelistic verse, but it's addressed to an established church. How does this change the concept of Jesus coming in and fellowshipping?

PRAYER

Dear God our Father, rescue us from coasting and cooling and even death. Send preachers and prophets to prod and correct us so that we may be faithful and useful to You, not living on the reputation of our past.

A GLIMPSE OF HEAVEN

Revelation 4–5

Jesus alone is worthy of our worship.

This last book of the New Testament, with all its symbolism, can seem difficult to understand. Theologians have examined it for centuries and still come to major differences in interpreting its meaning. Yet amid the complex imagery of this book stands one remarkably clear picture. It is a vision of Christ, our Redeemer, taking His rightful place of honor in heaven.

In our day, as in the days of John, the central figure of our faith can sometimes be sidelined amid debates over worship, church structure, the urgency of evangelism, or social concerns. While each of those discussions is important, none is primary. It is Jesus Christ, the Lamb of God, who stands at the center of our faith, who deserves our worship, and who should command our attention.

Revelation, comes from the Latin term *revelare*, which means to reveal. As the vision of Christ is revealed to you, you will be moved, like John, to stop and worship Him.

COMMENTARY

Revelation 4 and 5 are pivotal in the plot and structure of this book of the Bible. These chapters set the tone and precedent from the standpoint of heaven. They show us the preeminence of worship that precedes the judgments of the seven seals, bowls, and plagues. Everything of lasting value begins with worship. Joshua learned this before the conquest of Canaan (Josh. 5:13–15). Everything we do should arise out of and begin with the worship of God and the Lamb, who are worthy of our worship. Revelation 4 and 5 describe just how worthy the Godhead is.

WORDS FROM WESLEY
Revelation 4:1

Ch. 4. We are now entering on the main prophecy; the whole Revelation may be divided thus;
The 1st, 2nd, and 3rd chapters contain the introduction:
The 4th, and 5th, the proposition;
The 6th, 7th, 8th, and 9th, describe things which are already fulfilled;
The 10th–14th, things which are now fulfilling;
The 15th–19th, things which will be fulfilled shortly;
The 20th, 21st, 22nd, things at a greater distance. (ENNT)

The Father Is Worthy of Our Wholehearted Worship (Rev. 4)

Revelation 4:1 transports the reader from earth to heaven: **After this I looked, and there before me was a door standing open in heaven. And the voice I had first heard speaking to me like a trumpet said, "Come up here, and I will show you what must take place after this."** John's first-person description indicates he experienced what he saw and heard. Some assume a rapture of the church, but this is not the case. The assumption may fit a theology, but it may not square with Scripture. John is summoned to a revelation of a once-veiled mystery.

After this indicates a change of scenery—from earth to heaven. Heaven is the only stable location in the universe of Revelation. John was invited to enter through the open door to the most harmonious place that exists. We are taught to pray, "Your kingdom come, your will be done on earth as it is in heaven" (Matt. 6:10).

The open door represents access to an unveiled mystery. John was invited into the nerve center of the universe. The above/below perspective informs the reader that what occurs on earth in Revelation 6 through 19 has its origin in heaven. What John saw and heard informs us of our earthly situation, where the tyranny of the present obscures our view of God and distorts our perception of divine work all around us. While we may think evil is winning overwhelmingly, the viewpoint from heaven tells us evil cannot win. This perspective offers us a fresh vision that God reigns from heaven. God is in control of history, and God will soon stop evil.

The voice I had first heard speaking to me like a trumpet (4:1) is a reference to 1:10 but should not be associated with the voice of the Son of Man. The voice is an unidentified speaker within the narrative. In the Bible, trumpets are used to call or proclaim.

John was **in the Spirit** (v. 2) as he stated in 1:10. His point of view changed from earth below on Patmos to heaven above. He was in the throne room of heaven. The first thing John saw was **a throne in heaven with someone sitting on it** (4:2). The word order is significant. It is *what* he saw, then it is *who* he saw. The word **throne** appears fifty-five times in the New Testament, forty-one of those are in Revelation, suggesting the importance of God's sovereignty. God reigns in all majesty, power, and authority.

While the throne is not described, God is. The words **appearance** and **resembling** (v. 3) and **like** (vv. 6–7) indicate John was using the language of simile.

What John saw are colors. **And the one who sat there had the appearance of jasper and carnelian. A rainbow, resembling an emerald, encircled the throne** (v. 3). **Jasper** appears in several colors—red, brown, green, yellow. **Carnelian** can appear as a deep red, flesh red, or reddish white. The **rainbow** that **encircled** the **throne** is described as looking like an emerald, a rich green color. The picture is a beautiful blend of colors. This is the language of transcendence. An unveiling is taking place before John's eyes, but his description veils God. God is seen and yet not fully known. God is unfathomable and indescribable. John conveyed to us the mystery of God.

In verse 4, John looked away from God, and he saw **twenty-four other thrones, and seated on them were twenty-four elders.** Who are these elders? Some think the elders are angels, but this can't be the case, since in Revelation 7:11 angels and elders appear together. They are probably not the church, for the same verse suggests the redeemed are singing while the elders worship God. But the context of Revelation suggests they are kings. Revelation 4 has its counterpart in chapter 18. There kings mourn the fall of Babylon (Rev. 18:9). The elders wear **crowns of gold** (4:4) and can be viewed as kings. **White** reflects their inner being—pure and holy. However, their function is indisputable: They are part of an inner circle of servants associated with the throne room (see also 5:6; 14:3); they **worship** God (4:10; 5:8, 14; 11:16; 19:4); one points John to the Lamb (5:5); they **lay their crowns before the throne** (4:9–10); they sing God's praises (4:11; 5:9, 11–12); they hold harps, to play the music of the new song (5:8–10), and "golden bowls full of incense, which are the prayers of the saints" (5:8; compare Ps. 141:2), which reminds us no prayer is forgotten by God; and one elder explains the vast multitude that stands before the throne (7:9, 13–17).

WORDS FROM WESLEY

Revelation 4:8

This word (the word behind "Holy" in this verse) properly signifies separated, both in Hebrew and other languages. And when God is termed holy, it denotes that excellence, which is altogether peculiar to himself; and the glory flowing from all His attributes conjoined, shining forth from all His works, and darkening all things besides itself, whereby He is, and eternally remains, in an incomprehensible manner separate and at a distance, not only from all that is impure, but likewise from all that is created. (ENNT)

In a closer circle around the throne are **four living creatures** (4:6). The KJV calls them "beasts," perhaps partly because John described three of them as having faces like **a lion . . . an ox** and an **eagle** (v. 7). However, literally, these beings are simply the **living**. They are **covered with eyes, in front and in back** (v. 6), **eyes all around, even under** their **wings** (v. 8). The four living beings see God. They intimately know God. Their function is to worship and praise God and the Lamb (4:8–9; 5:8, 11, 14; 7:11; 19:4). They also have a role in the seal and bowl judgments (6:1, 3, 5, 7; 15:7).

Revelation 4 and 5 include five hymns of praise and worship. They are to the Father (4:8, 11), Christ the Lamb (5:9–10, 12), the Father and the Lamb (5:13). The four living beings are involved in all five hymns. Since they are closest to the throne, their worship exalts God as holy, the Almighty, and the fully present God. The worship of 4:11 exalts God as Creator of the cosmos. The rhetorical phrase **glory and honor and power** of verse 11 in concert with **holy, holy, holy** of verse 8 has the blessed Trinity in view. The four living never rest in their proclamation.

WORDS FROM WESLEY
Revelation 4:11

Worthy art thou to receive—This He receives not only when He is thus praised, but also when He destroys His enemies and glorifies himself anew; *the glory, and the honour, and the power*— Answering the thrice-holy of the living creatures, ver. 9. *For thou hast created all things*—Creation is the ground of all the works of God. Therefore for this, as well as for all His other works, will He be praised to all eternity. *And through thy will they were*— They began to be. It is to the free, gracious, and powerfully work-ing will of Him who cannot possibly need any thing, that all things owe their first existence. *And are created*—That is, continue in being ever since they were created. (ENNT)

The Lamb Is Worthy of Our Wholehearted Worship (Rev. 5)

The focal point of chapter 4 is the throne and the One seated on it. Chapter 5 has as its focal point the right hand of the One who sits on the throne. In the Father's **right hand** is **a scroll with writing on both sides and sealed with seven seals** (v. 1). **Right hand** is the only human-like description in the vision of God in chapters 4 and 5. The reference to God's right hand speaks of His supreme authority and sovereign power. The scroll is sealed shut by seven seals. Its contents are completely hidden. Only someone worthy is able to break its seals. The writing inside and out indicates nothing is left out or left unsaid. Everything will go completely as planned, and God will wrap up things on His terms.

The angel's proclamation raised a dilemma: **"Who is worthy to break the seals and open the scroll?"** (v. 2). None responded. John **wept** (v. 4). But **one of the elders** revived John's hope: **"Do not weep! See, the Lion of the tribe of Judah, the Root of David, has triumphed. He is able to open the scroll and its seven seals"** (v. 5). But when John turned to see the Lion, he saw **a Lamb, looking as if it had been slain, standing in the center of the throne** (v. 6). This vision of the standing Lamb suggests something has been completed and something else is commencing. Redemption has been completed. The Lamb is worthy to break the seals because He gave himself a "ransom for many" (Mark 10:45). Jesus' victory on the cross was not as a conquering general but as a sacrificial lamb. But this sacrifice is a form of strength. The event of the cross revealed God's power of salvation (Rom. 1:16). Jesus told Paul, "My grace is sufficient for you, for my power is made perfect in weakness" (2 Cor. 12:9). When we surrender to Jesus, His power empowers us for Christlike living.

The **seven horns and seven eyes** (Rev. 5:6) are symbols of Christ's immeasurable divine power and full knowledge of all things; He sees everything and knows everything. The number seven indicates the divine plenitude and completeness. **The seven spirits of God sent out into all the earth** (v. 6) is a reference to the Holy Spirit, whom the Father and Christ sent into the world (John 14:26; 15:26; 16:7).

WORDS FROM WESLEY
Revelation 5:6

And I saw—First, Christ in or on the midst of the throne; secondly, the four living creatures making the inner circle round Him, and thirdly, the four and twenty elders, making a larger circle round Him and them, *standing*—He lieth no more; He no more falls on His face; the days of His weakness and mourning are ended. He is now in a posture of readiness to execute all His offices of prophet, priest, and king; *as if he had been slain*—Doubtless with the prints of the wounds which He once received. And because He was slain, He is worthy to open the book (ver. 9), to the joy of His own people, and the terror of His enemies. *Having seven horns*—As a king, the emblem of perfect strength; *and seven eyes*—The emblem of perfect knowledge and wisdom. By these He accomplishes what is contained in the book, namely, by His almighty and all-wise Spirit. (ENNT)

The Lamb **took the scroll** out of the Father's hand (Rev. 5:7), and glorious worship and praise breaks out in heaven. The **four living . . . and the twenty-four elders fell down** (v. 8) in worship and **sang a new song** (v. 9). The song explains the worthiness of the Lamb, which is the theme of chapter 5. The Lamb is worthy to take the scroll and break its seals because He was slain. His shed blood is the basis of humanity's salvation. Christ's blood redeems us from the penalty of our sins and makes us **priests** to **God** (v. 10). **Priest** indicates the access the redeemed have to enter the presence of God and to offer the sacrifice of praise to Him (Heb. 13:15).

To the song of the four living and twenty-four elders is added another hymn of praise by **many angels, numbering thousands**

upon thousands, and ten thousand times ten thousand (v. 11). Their hymn exalts the Lamb with seven-fold praise: **power and wealth and wisdom and strength and honor and glory and praise** (v. 12). Still more voices praise the Lamb in verse 13: **every creature in heaven and on earth and under the earth and on the sea, and all that is in them**. All of heaven and earth praise God and the Lamb. **Amen** (v. 14) means so be it; in a fitting way, this word concludes the worship scene.

Chapter 5 begins with a narrow focal point of the scroll in the right hand of the Father, and as the chapter unfolds, John's view panned to an ever-widening panorama of concentric circles—from the Lamb to the four living to the twenty-four elders to the myriads of angels to the whole creation. The rhetorical sequence of seven worshipful descriptions in verse 12 exalts the Lamb in His perfection and plenitude. These combined sequences suggest the completeness of the salvation of humanity and the cosmos. God and the Lamb *are* worthy to receive the praise of the redeemed and all the hosts of heaven. In our worship services, let us not sit quietly, but praise and testify to His greatness.

WORDS FROM WESLEY

Revelation 5:13

This royal manifesto is, as it were, a proclamation, showing how Christ fulfills all things, *and every knee bows to him*, not only *on earth*, but also *in heaven and under the earth*. This book exhausts all things . . . and is suitable to a heart enlarged as the sand of the sea. It inspires the attentive and intelligent reader with such a magnanimity, that he accounts nothing in this world great, no, not the whole frame of visible nature, compared to the immense greatness of what he is here called to behold, yea, and in part to inherit. (ENNT)

DISCUSSION

Reflect on how much time you spend thinking about the future.

1. How can the church change its approach to Revelation from looking at it as a "crystal ball" to looking at it as Christ-centered?

2. God's presence at Mount Sinai—and here—is manifested in "flashes of lightning, rumblings and peals of thunder" (Rev. 4:5). Why would God present himself in that way?

3. Throughout Revelation 4, those around the throne proclaim "Holy, holy, holy is the Lord God Almighty." What is your definition of *holy*?

4. In Revelation 1, we see the physical characteristics of the Son. Now John described His character, attributes, and deeds (4:11). How do they match up?

5. The image of a lamb as a sacrifice threads its way through the entire Bible. Can you think of other passages that mention this? What are they about?

6. Why do you think Jesus is described in Revelation as both a lion and a lamb? How do you reconcile these very different images of the same person?

7. How does the "worthy" Lamb exhibit power? Wealth? Wisdom? Strength? Honor? Glory? Praise?

8. Praise appears to be the prime activity in heaven? How would you suggest that your church prepare its members for this?

PRAYER

O God, You are a mighty and majestic Father who has given us Your glorious and worthy Son to be our redemption. May we be worthy and faithful followers of the Lamb.

THE BEGINNING OF THE END

Revelation 6:1–17

No one will escape God's justice.

Our world has witnessed many natural catastrophes in recent years. Earthquakes, tornadoes, hurricanes, and tsunamis have devastated portions of the landscape. Terrorist activity has wreaked havoc in many places. Yet all of these events combined do not equal the devastation that is coming. In this study, the four horsemen of the Apocalypse begin the destruction that potentially affects 25 percent of humankind. How shall we respond? Do we have any hope?

One tendency is to withdraw into fear or isolation in response to the swirling events of the end times—and the seemingly random events of the present moment. These events are too grand, too powerful, and too overwhelming for us to alter. Many people feel a sense of helplessness about the future. Yet there is hope for those who are in Christ. Our hope is found in the Lamb—in His sacrifice that paid for our sins.

While the events described in Revelation may seem scary, properly understanding passages like the one at hand will produce just the opposite effect. They give us a sense of comfort because of the justice, power, and righteousness of God's judgment.

COMMENTARY

Revelation 4 and 5 set the context for chapter 6. Chapter 4 described John's vision of heaven's throne, the One who sat upon that throne, and the worshiping creatures (4:6–9) and elders (on their own secondary thrones; 4:4, 10) around *the* throne. Chapter 5 opens with a description of the One (Jesus Christ as Lord) sitting on the throne: He held "a scroll with writing on both sides and sealed with seven seals" (5:1). (In ancient times, seals were wax marks that kept unauthorized people from opening documents.)

In the midst of this regal group, a "mighty angel" (5:2) asked the identity of the authorized scroll-opener. After a period of John feeling overwhelming despair at not being able to answer that question, one of the creatures around the throne announced that the Lamb (the Lord and the Lamb were both the same—the glorified Jesus Christ) on the throne, the One holding the scroll, had earned the right to open the seals. That problem resolved, the group around the throne returned to singing their worship.

Within this extended picture, we, looking over John's shoulder, see the One who controls all events, including the scenes about to be portrayed by the opened seals.

The first four seals disclose four horses and their riders. Zechariah saw and described a similar picture (Zech. 6:1–8). In Zechariah's vision, the four horsemen represented God's judgment on Babylon, Egypt, and other nations that had oppressed God's people. This repetition of an ancient picture of judgment strongly hints that John's vision of four horses and riders (as well as the disasters portrayed in seals five and six) may also speak of God's judgment. The horsemen and their mounts may picture God's wrath to be poured out on evil forces in the end times yet to come. More likely, these riders represent forces God was allowing to ravage the earth even during John's lifetime, has allowed ever since the time of Jesus, and that earth's people will continue to experience until the end of time.

The Opening of the First Seal (Rev. 6:1–2)

As the first seal was broken, the invitation of the first creature brought forth from the scroll onto the stage of history **a white horse** (v. 2). What does this figure represent?

WORDS FROM WESLEY
Revelation 6:1

Before we proceed, it may be observed, 1. No man should constrain either himself or another, to explain every thing in this book. It is sufficient for every one to speak, just so far as he understands. 2. We should remember that although the ancient prophets wrote the occurrences of those kingdoms only with which Israel had to do, yet the Revelation contains what relates to the whole world through which the Christian church is extended. Yet, 3. We should not prescribe to this prophecy, as if it must needs admit or exclude this or that history, according as we judge one or the other, to be of great or small importance, God *seeth not as man seeth*. Therefore what we think great is often omitted, what we think little, inserted, in Scripture history or prophecy, 4. We must take care not to overlook what is already fulfilled; and not to describe as fulfilled what is still to come. (ENNT)

Revelation 19:11–12 offers a similar picture of a white horse and its rider. Since the white horse in chapter 19 is ridden by the Lord Jesus, many commentators assume these two pictures are identical, that the rider of the first seal is the Lord. This interpretation, however, does not fit this chapter's repeated pattern of destruction.

More likely, the first seal's white horse and rider represent military battle and conquest. (Roman generals celebrated victory by riding a white horse or a chariot pulled by several white horses in a triumphant parade.) The **bow** (6:2) carried by the rider arising from the first seal would add further weight to the idea that this first seal represents the lust for power and conquest visible in all wars of history.

The Opening of the Second Seal (Rev. 6:3–4)

Opening the second seal revealed a **fiery red** (v. 4) horse and its rider. If the white horse reflects the spirit behind human wars, this horse symbolizes the wars themselves. The white animal represents kings and counselors who plot for increased power as a result of war. The red portrays the blood that was shed by foot soldiers fighting the battles, as well as all the non-combatant civilians who suffer directly and indirectly through fierce battles.

Some Bible interpreters feel Jesus' prophecy of "wars and rumors of wars" (Mark 13:7) indicates that the number and severity of wars will increase as the end times approach. That may be true, but history has known few periods not plagued by this hobby of the powerful.

Historians call the centuries surrounding John's writing the *Pax Romana*, noting a period of Roman-dominated peace. But even during this time of relative tranquility, rebellions against Rome involved the deaths of hundreds of thousands. John's contemporaries saw the red horse frequently enough.

The Opening of the Third Seal (Rev. 6:5–6)

John's vision of the dreadful rainbow of horse colors continues with a **black horse** (v. 5). The inflated market prices of verse 6 clearly show this beast representing famine. **A quart of wheat** (v. 6) might feed one person. But if a man needs to work all day to earn enough to feed himself, how will he feed his family, not to mention provide for their other needs? This man might be able to buy **barley** at a better price, but even enough barley to feed his family on a workday leaves no food for the Sabbath or earnings to care for his family's housing or clothing.

The rider of the black horse carries **a pair of scales** (v. 5). The scales would involve two trays linked on a balance beam. The scales might relate to this passage's picture of measuring grain to be purchased as food, or perhaps the death angel weighing out how many people would perish in the black-horse famine. The final words about **oil** and **wine** (v. 6) indicate limits God placed on famine. Olive trees (producing olive oil) and grape vines, with deeper roots, might survive a short drought.

(See, for comparison, Gen. 43:11, where Jacob, even in the midst of famine, could send fruit to the Egyptian leaders.)

The black-horse famine, painful as it might be, would not destroy the human race, but offer a harsh reminder, at least for the poor, of God's sovereignty. The wealthy might have wine and oil, but what would the lower classes eat?

The Opening of the Fourth Seal (Rev. 6:7–8)

John next saw **a pale horse** (v. 8). The pure white horse offered a picture of glamour. In contrast, this pale grayish animal came in the color of death. The plagues offered in the first three seals resulted in the demise of a huge percentage of a region's people, represented by the figure of one-quarter. (This fraction does not indicate a precise proportion. Instead it demonstrates the severity of the suffering resulting from war, famine, and other dangers people have always faced and will continue to face until the end.) Ezekiel 14:21 gives the same list of God's dreadful judgments: "sword and famine and wild beasts and plague."

Within Jewish theology, *sheol* was the place of the shadowy dead. **Hades** (Rev. 6:8) is the Greek equivalent of *sheol*. The pale horse and his three predecessors certainly give the message that sin brings tragic results.

WORDS FROM WESLEY

Revelation 6:8

What has been already observed may be a fourfold proof, that the four horsemen, as with their first entrance in the reign of Trajan, which does by no means exhaust the contents of the four first seals, so with all their entrances in succeeding ages, and with the whole course of the world, and of visible nature, are in all ages subject to Christ, subsisting by His power, and serving His will, against the wicked and in defense of the righteous. (ENNT)

The Opening of the Fifth Seal (Rev. 6:9–11)

The suffering represented by the four horses would afflict not only sinners. Like the two criminals on crosses beside Jesus, they would be receiving what they had earned. But followers of Jesus, ones made righteous through the grace of God, would in John's lifetime as well as throughout the course of history also suffer grievously. Many men and women would be killed precisely because of their loyalty to Jesus. The fifth component of John's vision of the seals showed him many such martyrs. Suffering for Jesus' sake should never surprise His disciples. Jesus predicted that His followers would endure persecution for their devotion to Him. (See Mark 13:9–13; John 16:2.)

WORDS FROM WESLEY

Revelation 6:9

And when he opened the fifth seal—As the four former seals, so the three latter have a close connection with each other. These all refer to the invisible world; the fifth to the happy dead, particularly the martyrs; the sixth to the unhappy; the seventh to the angels, especially those to whom the trumpets are given. *And I saw*—Not only the church warring under Christ, and the world warring under Satan, but also the invisible hosts both of heaven and hell, are described in this book. And it not only describes the actions of both these armies upon earth, but their respective removals from earth, into a more happy or more miserable state, succeeding each other at several times, distinguished by various degrees, celebrated by various thanksgivings; and also the gradual increase of expectation and triumph in heaven, and of terror and misery in hell. (ENNT)

The vision disclosed by the fifth seal includes several meaningful details. John saw the **souls** of the martyrs **under the altar** (Rev. 6:9). (See Rev. 8:5 and 14:18 for other references to heaven's altar.) Within the God-ordained Old Testament worship, blood of sacrificed animals was poured out at the base of the altar. (See Lev. 17:11–14.) The fact that John's vision included the saints **under the altar** (Rev. 6:9) likely indicates that God sees the sacrifice of their lives as an offering to Him. The NIV text does not use the word *martyrs* in its description of **those who had been slain**, but the Greek word behind their **testimony** (*martyrian*) gives us the English word *martyr*.

WORDS FROM WESLEY

Revelation 6:11

And there was given to every one a white robe—An emblem of innocence, joy, and victory, in token of honour and favourable acceptance. *And it was said to them*—They were told how long. They were not left in that uncertainty, *that they should rest*—Should cease from crying. They rested from pain before, *a time*—This word has a peculiar meaning in this book, to denote which we may retain the original word *chronos*. Here are two classes of martyrs specified, the former killed under heathen Rome, the latter under papal Rome. The former are commanded to rest, till the latter are added to them. There were many of the former in the days of John: the first-fruits of the latter died in the thirteenth century. Now a time or chronos is 1111 years. This chronos began A. C. 98, and continued to the year 1209; or from Trajan's persecution, to the first crusade against the Waldenses, *Till*—It is not said, immediately after this time is expired, vengeance shall be executed: but only, that immediately after this time, their brethren and fellow-servants will come to them. This event will precede the other, and there will be some space between. (ENNT)

John heard the martyrs crying out to God, asking when He would punish those who opposed His people. Their prayer echoes the anguish of the psalmist (Ps. 79:5–10). The opponents are described as **the inhabitants of the earth** (Rev. 6:10), a phrase occurring frequently in Revelation to describe those who reject God's ways. (See 3:10; 8:13; 11:10; 13:8, 12; 17:2, 8.) Perhaps in a search for justice, the martyrs' patience was running low, but even so, they respectfully recognized the One to whom they appealed as the **Sovereign Lord** of holiness and truth.

How did God respond to the martyrs' plea? In action and with a promise. John saw each of the martyrs receiving **a white robe** (v. 11). Throughout Revelation, such garments denote God's favor and purity. (See 3:5, 18; 4:4; 7:9, 13; 19:14.) God would in His time cause the evil to receive punishment for their crimes, but that time had not yet come. God held a plan that would work out for the best, even if not immediately, and even if not preventing the pain of other disciples.

The Opening of the Sixth Seal (Rev. 6:12–14)

This portion of John's extended vision continued as the Lord Jesus opened a sixth seal. What did the opening of this seal reveal? The day of God's wrath (6:17). The day the martyrs pled for, when God would avenge the suffering of His faithful servants. To portray this horror, the vision God gave John included what original readers would have recognized as the common symbols of the end of time. What dread pictures did God employ? Should we take these pictures literally? Perhaps. Would God use other pictures if we were communicating the end of time to twenty-first-century readers? Perhaps.

A great earthquake (v. 12). Old Testament prophets had portrayed God visiting the earth or the end of time in terms of great shattering of the earth. (See Ex. 19:18; Isa. 2:19; Amos 8:8; Ezek. 38:19; Joel 2:10, 31; Hag. 2:6.) The greatest of prophets also mentioned coming earthquakes (Matt. 24:7).

Darkening of the **sun** and **moon** (Rev. 6:12). (Compare Amos 8:9; Isa. 13:13; 50:3; Ezek. 32:7; 38:19; Joel 2:31.) Jesus used this imagery as well in Matthew 24:29. The reference to **sackcloth made of goat hair** (Rev. 6:12) may indicate the best quality sackcloth, dense enough to cover even the light of the sun. A moon of **blood red** color would hardly be visible in the night sky.

The falling of the **stars** (v. 13). Apocryphal books (with which the first readers of Revelation would have been familiar) used this image frequently. It appears also in the Old Testament and Gospels. (See Isa. 34:4; Nah. 3:12; Matt. 24:29.) Those experiencing simultaneous shaking of the earth and total darkness would freeze in terror. The steadiness of the earth and the light that enables vision—two elements all people have taken for granted—would be removed.

The **sky . . . rolling up . . . like a scroll** (v. 14). (Compare Isa. 34:4; Ps. 102:25–26.) Picture spreading out a tightly rolled document. If you were then to let it go, it would spring back into its original position.

Every mountain and island disappearing (v. 14). (Compare Jer. 4:24; Nah. 1:5.) We may perhaps connect this tragedy with the earthquakes. When God comes to judge, nothing outside himself can be considered secure.

The Response of Earth's People (Rev. 6:15–17)

When God reveals His wrath on evil, ordinary people (**slave** and **free man** [v. 15]) will run for shelter. But even those who depend on their position or possessions for security will find themselves defenseless. As people in Noah's day climbed as high as they could to escape the rising waters, others in the time of God's judgment will seek the best shelter they can find. In the first century, people would have run for **caves** (v. 15). (Compare the caves near the Dead Sea where ancient Jews hid scrolls that would remain safe for nearly two thousand years.) In the horror of John's vision, people preferred immediate death (**mountains** and **rocks** [v. 16] falling on them) to the prospect of prolonged suffering. (For Old Testament foreshadowing of this fear, see Isa. 13:6, 8; Zeph. 1:14; Joel 2:1, 11; Hos. 10:8.) From what and whom would these people be fleeing? **The wrath of the Lamb** (v. 16)—the Lamb whose anger melts into love when sinners turn and run to Him, rather than away from Him.

DISCUSSION

No matter how we may individually interpret some of the images or events described in Revelation, we can learn important lessons.

1. What do you believe is the source of these four destructive horses? Do they originate with God, the sinful world, or the Enemy?

2. What does the Lamb's power to unleash the four horses tell you about God's control of human events?

3. What interpretations have you heard for white horse? What signs of its activity are apparent today?

4. How are the red and black horses traditionally interpreted? What signs of its activity are apparent today?

5. How is the pale horse traditionally interpreted? What signs of its activity are apparent today?

6. Have you ever wondered how long it will be until God finally judges the injustice on earth? Do the events described here give you more or less confidence that God's justice will come "soon"?

7. What do you think we should be doing while we wait for God's justice to appear? Ignoring injustice? Working to bring justice? Simply waiting?

8. How do you know you are ready to stand before God and be judged?

PRAYER

Dear God, our mighty and fearsome Father in heaven, vengeance is Yours alone, but by Your grace You are slow to anger. Give even more time to those who hate You, so that they may turn from their wicked ways, repent, and cast themselves upon Your mercy.

THE ULTIMATE VICTORY CELEBRATION

Revelation 7:9–17

A great celebration awaits the faithful.

What does the word *heaven* mean to you? Do you picture a place where wispy angels and shadowy spirits flit back and forth, playing harps? Perhaps you picture your most ideal setting—a trout stream where you can fish uninterrupted for days on end or a shopping mall where all the items are free. Most of us take our images of heaven either from popular culture or from our own imagination. Yet John's vision reveals heaven to be something different from what we typically imagine. Heaven is a place of joy and celebration!

While the subject of celebratory worship can evoke tensions here on earth, any controversy over worship styles will vanish as we stand before the throne of God himself in heaven. There, worshipers are intent on exalting the Lamb of God, whose blood has redeemed them and given them the ultimate victory over sin, self, Satan, and death. They celebrate victory through the blood of the Lamb. And someday we will join them!

This study gives us a glimpse of the celebration that awaits the people of God who have persevered through the trials of this earth. As we use our imaginations to picture this grand event, we'll gain a better perspective on the temporary events we endure here on earth and will gain a greater longing for heaven— our real home.

COMMENTARY

The pictures presented in the last study and this one could not be more different. Revelation 6 describes dispensing wrath, as the four horsemen ride out to punish the earth for its wickedness in the sight of holy God. The slain Lamb of chapter 5 is the agent of this destruction, opening six of seven seals that produce conquest, war, famine, death, earthquakes and cosmic disturbances, and terror for all of humanity. Furthermore, the servants of God are being martyred during this period, "slain because of the word of God and the testimony they had maintained" (Rev. 6:9). In John's vision, these souls take refuge under the altar of God, imploring that their deaths be avenged. They are given white robes and told to wait until all the saints destined for martyrdom have been killed. The chapter ends with the plea of humanity to the earth: "Fall on us and hide us from the face of him who sits on the throne and from the wrath of the Lamb! For the great day of their wrath has come, and who can stand?" (6:16–17).

WORDS FROM WESLEY

Revelation 7:9

A great multitude—Of those who had happily finished their course. Such multitudes are afterward described, and still higher degrees of glory which they attain, after a sharp fight and magnificent victory, ch. 14:1; 15:2; 19:1; 20:4. There is an inconceivable variety in the degrees of reward in the other world. Let not any slothful one say, If I get to heaven at all, I will be content? such an one may let heaven go altogether. In worldly things men are ambitions to get as high as they can. Christians have a far more noble ambition. The difference between the very highest and the lowest state in the world, is nothing to the smallest difference between the degrees of glory. But who has time to think of this? Who is at all concerned about it? *Standing before the throne*—in the full vision of God, *and palms in their hands*— Tokens of joy and victory. (ENNT)

The tone of judgment and wrath shifts in chapter 7, and the terrified question of humanity at the end of the previous chapter is answered. Who can stand before God and the Lamb? The saints in white who were previously huddled under the altar are now "standing before the throne and in front of the Lamb" (v. 9), worshiping and praising God for salvation through Jesus' blood.

WORDS FROM WESLEY
Revelation 7:14

All unprejudiced persons may see with their eyes, that He is already renewing the face of the earth: And we have strong reason to hope that the work He hath begun, He will carry on unto the day of the Lord Jesus; that He will never intermit this blessed work of His Spirit, until He has fulfilled all His promises, until He hath put a period to sin, and misery, and infirmity, and death, and reestablished universal holiness and happiness, and caused all the inhabitants of the earth to sing together, "Hallelujah, the Lord God omnipotent reigneth!" "Blessing, and glory, and wisdom, and honour, and power, and might, be unto our God for ever and ever!" (Rev. 7:12). (WJW, vol. 6, 288)

Yes, "the Lamb of God, who takes away the sin of the world" (John 1:29), Jesus Christ, is an agent of God's destruction, but He is also an instrument of God's love, providing salvation—deliverance from wrath—for those who "have washed their robes and made them white in the blood of the Lamb" (Rev. 7:14). This chapter describes His victory, the tidal turn in the cosmic struggle, and the regeneration and renewal for the people of God resulting from the shedding of His blood. Because of our hope in Jesus Christ, we can join the throng, singing joyfully, "Salvation belongs to our God, who sits on the throne, and to the Lamb" (v. 10)!

WORDS FROM WESLEY
Revelation 7:14

These are they—Not martyrs; for these are not such a multitude as no man can number. But as all the angels appear here, so do all the souls of the righteous, who had lived from the beginning of the world, who *come*—He does not say, Who did come. But who come now also; to whom likewise pertain all who will come hereafter, *out of great affliction*—Of various kinds, wisely and graciously allotted by God to all His children, *and have washed their robes*—From all guilt, *and made them white*—In all holiness, *by the blood of the Lamb*—Which not only cleanses, but adorns us also. (ENNT)

Imagery of the Passage (Rev. 7:9–17)

The imagery of apocalyptic literature is important, because it is the author's attempt to express the inexpressible. The author's words paint a portrait of God, who has no form, so we can "see" God. Every word, therefore, helps us gain elements of the scene in his mind. In this chapter, we see many facets of the Father and the Son.

God (Rev. 7:9–12, 15–17)

The first impression we have of God in Revelation is that God is the King. Throughout the previous chapters and this one, John referred to God as the One **who sits on the throne** (vv. 10, 15; 4:2, 3, 9; 5:1, 7, 13). Perhaps this descriptor is used so frequently to remind the audience, who lived during a time when the Roman emperors ruled Palestine, that God is *truly* king. Roman emperors may come and go, occupying earthly thrones, but God in heaven *sits* firmly on *the* throne. He is the true and eternal King of Kings.

God is perfect and worthy of praise. In apocalyptic literature, numbers are important, particularly the number seven, which represents perfection. In previous chapters, hymns contain words of praise in combinations of three, four, and seven. In this chapter, the number again is seven, indicating perfect praise for a perfect

Being: **Praise and glory and wisdom and thanks and honor and power and strength be to our God for ever and ever** (v. 12).

God is Lord of the past, present, and future. The scene describes God as the King of the present and future. However, many aspects of this description allude to God's activity in the Old Testament. First, several prophetic books contain descriptions of the heavenly throne that bear similarities with what we read in Revelation (see Isa. 6; Ezek. 1). Second, the elder remarks that **he who sits on the throne will spread his tent over them** (v. 15), a reminder of the tabernacle in which the Israelites worshiped before the temple was built. Third, the **great multitude that no one could count** (v. 9) reminds us of God's promise to Abraham in Genesis 15:5.

God is Master, Healer, and Provider. Those wearing white robes will stand **before the throne of God and serve him day and night in his temple** (v. 15). They will never again be separated from their Lord. God will **spread his tent over them**, meaning He will take care of all their needs. They will never again be hungry, thirsty, or hot (v. 16), filled with grief, pain-stricken, or burdened with the cares of the world: **And God will wipe away every tear from their eyes** (v. 17).

Jesus (Rev. 7: 9–10, 14, 17)

Jesus is also portrayed in this scene as a victorious King. The first allusion to His victory is the mention of the **palm branches** the martyrs are holding **in their hands** (v. 9). When Jesus entered Jerusalem in the final days of His life, He was greeted by people waving palm branches, used in celebrations of victory. And **the Lamb** is described as existing **at the center of the throne** (v. 17), indicating He is one with God, the King.

Jesus Is Savior. This multitude formerly under the altar was given white robes (6:9–11), a symbol of blessedness and purity.

This text tells us these martyrs **have washed their robes and made them white in the blood of the Lamb** (7:14), who was described earlier as "slain" (5:6). The martyrs praise God and the Lamb, crying loudly, **Salvation belongs to our God, who sits on the throne, and to the Lamb** (7:10). Salvation comes only through the blood of the Lamb.

WORDS FROM WESLEY
Revelation 7:17

For the Lamb will feed them—With eternal peace and joy, so that they shall hunger no more, *and will lead them to living fountains of water*—The comforts of the Holy Spirit, so that they shall thirst no more. Neither shall they suffer or grieve any more: *For God will wipe away all tears from their eyes.* (ENNT)

Jesus Is the Shepherd. In an unusual twist of imagery, the slain Lamb becomes the Shepherd for others (7:17)! As the caring Shepherd who takes care of His sheep in the heat of the day, **he will lead them to springs of living water** (v. 17). This picture takes us to Psalm 23, describing the actions of God as a Shepherd to His flock: taking care of their needs; providing green pastures for rest and cool, clear water for their thirst; and leading them safely through danger and evil.

These depictions of God and Jesus provide a refreshing change after the wrath and terror of the previous chapter. The holy God who must punish sin is also a God of hope, providing a way out from wrath and destruction.

The Hymns (Rev. 7:12)

Many times our eyes slide over sections of the Bible that appear to be poetry; we want to get right to the action. However, words of worship or hymns are used so frequently in Revelation they must serve a purpose. An examination regarding differences in four of these similar hymns could be profitable.

The nouns used in these hymns are interesting, because four we can easily see are traits God possesses: **wisdom**, **strength**, wealth, and **power** (v. 12). At least two of the others generally express offerings given to God—**praise** and **thanks**—while the terms **glory** and **honor** could fall into both categories.

The Great Tribulation (Rev. 7:14)

The term **great tribulation** (v. 14), sometimes translated as the "great ordeal," is interpreted differently by scholars of the Bible, ranging from the general to the specific.

Because of the symbolic nature of apocalyptic literature, many people regard the term as a way of describing the persecution of God's people over the course of history.

A second interpretive method is based on the primary purpose of apocalyptic literature, to encourage those undergoing great hardships, reminding them evil will eventually be defeated by good. John, for example, was writing to Christians experiencing persecution meted out by one of the Roman emperors known to be antagonistic to Christianity, such as Nero or Domitian. A number of images can be interpreted as references to Rome. John's message is that although Satan may seem to be in control of the world, God is the true victor; Christians must remain strong to the end. Thus, these scholars would argue that the book has a specific purpose for a specific time in history.

A third perspective is that the great tribulation is a specific period of time at the end of the world when there will be a persecution of Christians more severe than any other experienced. These scholars take the term literally, emphasizing the word *great* and the definite article *the*. This view, they believe, is supported by Daniel 12, which mentions "a time of distress such as has not happened from the beginning of nations until then" (12:1).

The length and description of this period of time is another point of conjecture among biblical scholars, who use the calculations given in Daniel 8:14 and 12:11–12, as well as details scattered throughout the books of the New Testament, as support for various arguments regarding the sequence of events at the end of the world. However, since Daniel is also an example of apocalyptic literature, written during a period of severe persecution against the Jews by the Roman emperor Antiochus Epiphanes in the second or third century B.C., some would argue that its details refer solely to the past.

These are only a few of the many theories regarding this subject, which have spawned books, charts, and even movies, not to mention arguments, division, and rancor. Although it may be interesting to examine prophecies of the end times and conjecture how current events may play into them, Revelation is not merely a puzzle with details to be twisted and sifted through. The primary purpose of Revelation is to provide encouragement through times of suffering and hope for the future. God is on His throne. The Lamb has overcome. Our future on this earth and in heaven is safely in God's hands. Therefore, praise and glory and wisdom and thanks and honor and power and strength *are now* and *will be* our God's forever and ever.

DISCUSSION

Pray for Christians who are suffering for their faith today.

1. John received his revelation during one of the bloodiest and most gruesome persecutions of Christians. How would his message give them hope?

2. Who was vying for "praise and glory" during the period when John wrote? Who is vying for it today?

3. Who was vying for "wisdom and thanks and honor" then? Now?

4. Who was vying for "power and strength" then? Now?

5. How might this passage give encouragement for people living under a repressive regime? What does it say to you?

6. How do you reconcile the image of the wrathful Lamb in the previous study and today's image of the kind Shepherd?

7. How do verses 16 and 17 offer hope to our brothers and sisters facing persecution today?

8. What is the value of looking to the future? What can future vision do for you? What can't it do?

9. In what ways could Christians who are not being persecuted offer support or help to those who are facing it?

10. In what specific ways have you sensed God protection and provision over you?

PRAYER

God our Father and King, we yearn for the day when all Christians will be as one people gathered around Your throne to glorify the Lamb and the Father. Bring to us now a greater unity of spirit to prepare us for that day.

7

CHRIST WINS; SATAN LOSES

Revelation 11:15–19; 12:7–12

We can overcome the world by the power of Christ.

How would your life change if you could know the future? Many people stake their fortune on guessing what the future holds. Stock market investors, sports gamblers, and insurance agents all risk an investment against the hoped-for outcome of future events. Sometimes they win. Sometimes they lose.

In this study, we board a time machine and learn the outcome of a cosmic conflict and which of the opponents will ultimately be victorious. The study begins with the seventh angel sounding the seventh trumpet. The sounding of this trumpet signals the beginning of the reign of Christ over heaven and earth. Although Christians may differ in their interpretation of when that event has happened or will happen, they all agree on this: The outcome of the battle is already known—Christ wins; Satan loses.

The result of that victory can be felt now, not just at some future date. Because we know that Jesus is the ultimate champion, we can live every day with greater confidence. In spiritual terms, the future is now.

COMMENTARY

Revelation is complex and filled with symbols. Already we have seen God's wrath being poured out on the earth as the seven seals of the scroll are opened. When the seventh seal is broken, seven angels are given seven trumpets to declare the coming of even more judgments from the throne of God.

It is hard for us to understand God's wrath, because in Christ we will be spared from it. However, one day God's wrath will be poured out on all those who have rejected Him. As awful as this day will be for unbelievers, it will be a day of victory for those in Christ Jesus.

The Seventh Trumpet Sounds (Rev. 11:15)

In this passage, an angel in heaven sounds the final or seventh trumpet announcing another judgment upon the earth. The seventh trumpet is used to usher in the bowl judgments that complete God's wrath upon those who refused to repent and believe.

WORDS FROM WESLEY
Revelation 11:15

The kingdom of the world—That is, the royal government over the whole world and all its kingdoms, Zech. 14:9 *is become the kingdom of our Lord*—This province has been in the enemy's hands: it now returns to its rightful Master. In the Old Testament, from Moses to Samuel, God himself was the king of His own people. And the same will be in the New Testament: He will himself reign over the Israel of God: *and of his Christ*—. . . Prophets and priests were anointed, but more especially kings: whence that term *the anointed*, is applied only to a king. Accordingly, whenever the Messiah is mentioned in Scripture, His kingdom is implied. *Is become*—In reality all things (and so the kingdom of the world) are God's in all ages. Yet Satan and the present world, with its kings and lords, are risen against the Lord and against His Anointed. God now puts an end to this monstrous rebellion, and maintains His right to all things. And this appears in an entirely new manner, as soon as the seventh angel sounds. (ENNT)

In Scripture trumpets are used for various purposes. Trumpets (or *shofar*) were sounded to declare the beginning of feasts or festivals such as the Sabbath and the new year (Feast of Trumpets). Trumpets were sounded to call God's people to repentance, such as on the Day of Atonement (Lev. 23:24; Num. 10:10). Trumpets were sounded to declare the Year of Jubilee when slaves were released and debts were cancelled (Lev. 25:9). They were also used to call God's people to battle (Joel 2:1). And trumpets were blown at the accession of a king to his throne (1 Kings 1:33–34).

This seventh trumpet is a culmination of all these. It is a call to worship and repentance, an alarm that the release of the captives is at hand, a warning of impending war, and the accession of a new King. When the seventh trumpet blasts, an announcement is made: **The kingdom of the world has become the kingdom of our Lord and of his Christ, and he will reign for ever and ever** (Rev. 11:15). At that time, Christ will rule over the earth, and He alone will be worshiped. This is the fulfillment of what Daniel prophesied: the establishing of God's eternal kingdom (see Dan. 2:44).

A Time of Evaluation (Rev. 11:16–19)

The twenty-four elders react to the sounding of this trumpet by worshiping before God's throne. Some believe these elders represent the twelve patriarchs and the twelve disciples—representing the old and new covenants. Others believe they correspond to the twenty-four divisions of priests and Levites who led Israel in worship (see 1 Chron. 24–25). Regardless who they are, their reaction to this announcement is that of total worship. We see them leaving their thrones and falling **on their faces** in humility before almighty God (Rev. 11:16).

Giving thanks, they declare the fact that God is worthy to be worshiped because He has **great power** and has **begun to reign** (v. 17). This does not mean God was powerless prior to this point, but that He has now begun to release His power on the evil of the world through judgment. This final trumpet unleashes God's wrath upon earth through the bowl judgments that affect the earth, sea, water, air, and all those who have rebelled against Him.

WORDS FROM WESLEY
Revelation 7:17

The Almighty—He who hath all things in His power as the only Governor of them, *who is, and who was*—God is frequently styled, He who is, and who was, and who is to come. But now He is actually come, the words, *who is to come*, are, as it were, swallowed up. When it is said, we thank thee that thou hast taken thy great power, it is all one as, we thank thee that thou art come. . . . *Thou hast taken thy great power*—This is the beginning of what is done under the trumpet of the seventh angel. God has never ceased to use His power: but He has suffered His enemies to oppose it, which He will now suffer no more. (ENNT)

However, not all respond to God's power and rule in this fashion. **The nations were angry; and your wrath has come** (v. 18). Those in rebellion to God respond with anger rather than worship. As the wrath of God is poured out on the earth via the plagues, the hearts of those living in rebellion to God become more callous. Their refusal to repent puts them at greater risk until they are unable to see the wisdom of turning from sin and turning to God. This is a reminder to be careful that we do not refuse the conviction of God's Spirit and end up with hard hearts.

This sounding of the seventh trumpet is also a time of evaluation, a time **for judging the dead** (v. 18). This includes the unrighteous as well as Old and New Testament **saints**. However, we must understand that believers and unbelievers will face different judgments for different reasons.

Unbelievers will face judgment for their sins at what is called the great white throne judgment. They will stand before the Lord as the books of their lives are opened. At this judgment, they will understand all their good deeds are insufficient to save them. They will also see that because of their rejection of Christ, their names are not written in the Book of Life. They will then be cast into the lake of fire. (See Rev. 20:11–15.)

Believers will not face this judgment. Jesus said those who believe in Him will have eternal life and do not come into this judgment (John 5:24). Jesus condemned sin on the cross, and those who believe in Him are spared this condemnation because we are in Christ Jesus (Rom. 8:1–4). However, believers will face Christ and receive an evaluation. Second Corinthians 5:10 says we must all appear before the judgment seat of Christ. Believers will be judged on our deeds, not to determine whether we will go to heaven but to determine rewards. As Jesus sits on the judgment seat, He will reward those who were faithful to Him throughout their earthly lives. We will be given imperishable rewards (see 1 Cor. 9:25). Jesus is coming again and is bringing His reward with Him to render to each believer according to what we have done (see Rev. 22:12).

God's Response (Rev. 11:19)

As the seventh trumpet is sounded and worship begins, God responds in heaven and on earth. In the beginning of Revelation 11, John was instructed to measure the temple on earth, including those who worship there. Here we see that there is not only a temple on earth but another in heaven. We see **God's temple in heaven was opened** (v. 19). This is significant when we understand only the priests could enter into the earthly temple. This temple had two rooms. The first was the Holy Place, where the golden menorah, table of showbread, and the altar of incense stood. Beyond that there was the Most Holy Place (Holy of Holies), which housed the ark of the covenant. In Old Testament times, only the high priest could enter the Most Holy Place, and only once a year on the Day of Atonement. On the day Jesus died, the dividing curtain between these two rooms was torn in two, indicating the way was now open for everyone at any time.

Here in Revelation, the heavenly temple John saw did not have a curtain torn in two, but it was opened so wide that **within his temple was seen the ark of his covenant** (v. 19). The ark of the covenant was Israel's symbol of God's presence and His covenant relationship with them. The ark of the covenant was considered the throne of God. The opening of this heavenly temple signifies all the promises of God are fulfilled, and He will sit upon His throne for all to see.

The temple opening initiated a series of natural phenomena, including **flashes of lightning, rumblings, peals of thunder, an earthquake and a great hailstorm** (v. 19). In Revelation an earthquake accompanies the last of each of the series of judgments: when the final seal was broken (8:5), here at the seventh trumpet, and also at the last bowl judgment (16:18–21). Some have called these earthquakes the "signature of God" upon all that has been said by the twenty-four elders in 11:16–18.

War in Heaven (Rev. 12:7–9)

This passage gives us details of Satan's eviction from heaven. Some believe this is the record of Satan's expulsion from heaven before the creation of man. However, given the context, others believe this event takes place after that point. Revelation 12:4–5 describe the persecution of Christ at His birth and His ascension into heaven. If we read verses 7–9 in this context, this war in heaven seems to occur between Christ's first and second coming to earth, when He will rule with a rod of iron.

Regardless, we see a war between Michael, who in Scripture is described as an archangel and protector of God's people (see Dan. 10:13; Jude 9), and the dragon (Satan) and his angels (demons). They were not strong enough to overtake Michael and the heavenly host, so **the great dragon was hurled down** (Rev. 12:9) from heaven to earth. The language here seems to indicate that at this point Satan increases his activity to deceive and destroy.

The verse goes on to describe the dragon as none other than **that ancient serpent called the devil, or Satan** (v. 9). We know it was the serpent who deceived Eve in the garden. This serpent was called the Devil. **Devil** means "slanderer." He is also called **Satan**, "accuser." This accuser roams the earth looking for those weak in faith. He is seeking those he can devour (1 Pet. 5:8–9). His goal is to lead **the whole world astray** (Rev. 12:9).

Satan continues to slander and accuse us, keeping many believers defeated. We must remember that even though we have a powerful Enemy who has an army of supporters, we have a greater power within us that will help us to overcome him.

They Overcame the Enemy (Rev. 12:10–12)

A hymn of praise begins to resonate from heaven: **Now have come the salvation and the power and the kingdom of our God, and the authority of his Christ** (v. 10). This is a shout of victory over this Enemy. The word **salvation** here does not just mean our salvation from sin and entrance to heaven, but our rescue from Satan's clutches.

The hymn continues praising God, saying that **the accuser of our brothers . . . has been hurled down** (v. 10). We know from the story of Job that prior to this Satan had access to heaven to accuse the righteous before the throne of God (Job 1:6–7). Now his access is denied.

We have nothing to fear, because the power to overcome our enemy is within our hands. There are three aspects to this ultimate victory over Satan. First is the power of **the blood of the Lamb** (Rev. 12:11). Christ's sacrifice on the cross is the basis for overcoming the Devil. Therefore those who personally accept this sacrifice enter in to the victory of Christ over death, hell, and Satan. Second, they overcame by **the word of their testimony** (v. 11). Those who accept Jesus' sacrifice on the cross confirm this by what they say. Romans 10:10 tells us with our hearts we believe, but it is when we are not afraid to testify to others that we experience God's full salvation. Third, an overcomer is one who has set his or her fears aside and is willing to step out in faith. These believers **did not love their lives so much as to shrink from death** (Rev. 12:11). When we die to ourselves, we begin to experience God's overcoming power. This can refer to dying to our selfish desires and living for God, or it may be a call to completely give up our physical lives for the cause of Christ.

We have a powerful Enemy who should not be minimized. He is dangerous **because he knows that his time is short** (v. 12). Satan understands he is a defeated foe who has a limited amount of time until his final destruction (20:10). Although he is a formidable foe, we have nothing to fear, because the power of God is greater—and that power resides in us. Let us walk in that power and rejoice that in Christ we are victorious!

WORDS FROM WESLEY

Revelation 12:12

But let him who does not take these warnings for senseless outcries and blind alarms, beg of God with all possible earnestness, to give him His heavenly light herein. (ENNT)

DISCUSSION

We can have peace to know that in Christ, we are victorious, and Satan has no hold on us!

1. What makes a good dramatic hero? In what ways is Jesus like that in these verses?

2. Describe the challenge He faces?

3. How is the Enemy described? Do you see characteristics of this Enemy in worldly leaders?

4. What evil does Christ defeat? What injustices does He right? What evil and injustices do we face today?

5. Keep in mind, Revelation may have been written for multiple audiences. In the first century, historically, who might have been considered the "dragon"? What battles were Christians facing then?

6. Revelation can also be understood both as symbolism for the struggle of good verses evil as well as prophecy of future events. How does this section encourage you in the struggles you face?

7. Read verse 11:17 aloud. How has the Lord God Almighty begun to reign today?

PRAYER

Dear God our Father, we look forward to the day when Satan will be finally and forever a defeated foe and Your reign will be total and complete over the whole universe. But until then, may Your reign be total and complete over us.

8

A HEAVENLY PERSPECTIVE ON EARTH

Revelation 13:1–18

You can know that your name is written in the Lamb's Book of Life.

As you pull back the curtain to watch the calamitous end-times events unfold, do not fail to hear the central message of this incredible prophecy: We must remain faithful to Jesus and place our hope in Him. We can have confidence in Christ regardless of the chaotic and frightening events that the future may hold.

While it is difficult to say precisely who or what the imagery described in this study represents, the passage does give a grand overview of the events surrounding the end of time. We know there will be powerful people. There will be turmoil. There will be disastrous events. Yet the Lord of all will emerge victorious.

COMMENTARY

Revelation 13 contains many of the things people associate with Revelation: the beasts, the mark, and the number 666. However, before discussing the content of these verses, we ought to review some of the characteristics of Revelation as a whole.

First, it is important to remember Revelation is apocalyptic literature. Apocalyptic literature was usually written by members of groups who were experiencing persecution. Its writers often use exaggerated imagery to make their point in clear, shocking ways. This kind of writing flourished among Jews and Christians during the Roman occupation of Israel. While under the Romans, both groups used apocalyptic writings to encourage people to stand firm in their faith in the midst of difficult times.

Second, it is important to remember that the images used in this chapter—though they might legitimately be applied to current figures and events—were first used to describe the author's historical situation. In John's case, they appear to describe the Roman Empire and its state-sponsored religion of emperor worship. The cities in Asia Minor Jesus addressed through John in his letters were administrative centers in the Roman Empire, and, perhaps in an effort to gain favor with the Romans, their citizens wholeheartedly endorsed the emperor cult and opposed Christians who, by their lack of participation, sullied the impression of their cities' loyalty to the emperor.

John probably wrote during the reign of the emperor Domitian, sometime around A.D. 95. Historians tell us that Domitian eagerly embraced the emperor cult as a way of extending and solidifying his power. Furthermore, Domitian's reign was marked by intermittent local persecutions of the church, most notably in western Asia Minor, and it is probable Revelation addresses this situation.

Finally, it is important to consider how this chapter functions within the book's larger argument. While the book as a whole attempts to encourage persecuted Christian communities, chapters 12–14 further that goal by telling the story of the church's battle against its foes in terms of a battle between the monsters of evil and the armies of God. God will win that battle, and the church is reminded that even in the midst of persecution, it is called to serve and worship God alone, despite the cost.

The Beast from the Sea (Rev. 13:1–10)

Keeping these points in mind, we begin our discussion by noting the battle is already raging and "the dragon . . . went off to make war against . . . those who obey God's commandments" (12:17). The battle intensifies in chapter 13 with **a beast coming out of the sea** (v. 1). Much ink has been spilled in an effort to understand the beast's **ten horns and seven heads** (v. 1). Many scholars feel John was referring to the Roman Empire—with the ten horns representing its emperors and the seven heads the seven hills upon which the city sat. The image of the wounded head that has been healed (v. 3) supports that argument as a reference to the Emperor Nero who, after committing suicide, was buried without a public funeral. Since the people did not see his corpse, rumors circulated around the empire for many years that Nero would return to life and claim his throne. John's readers would, perhaps, have seen that allusion to Nero as confirmation that this beast did refer to the empire.

Verse 2 then goes on to describe the beast in terms reminiscent of the beasts Daniel saw in his vision. However, while Daniel used those images to describe four different beasts, John combined them, creating a composite portrait of evil incarnate. It's as if he took all the images other writers used to describe those who opposed God and combined them in this one stunning beast. The beast here refers specifically to the Roman Empire, but John's creative use of Daniel's imagery allows this chapter's story to be the timeless story of all demonic forces that have stood against God's work and His purposes. It invites us to place ourselves inside that story as we consider the things that strive to pull our allegiance away from God.

WORDS FROM WESLEY

Revelation 13:1

O reader! This is a subject wherein we also are deeply concerned: and which must be treated, not as a point of curiosity, but as a solemn warning from God. The danger is near. Be armed, both against force and fraud, even with the whole armour of God. (ENNT)

This sea beast is a servant of the dragon, and verse 2 tells us the **dragon gave the beast his power and his throne and great**

authority. We then see how the sea beast, by means of a miraculous healing of a fatal wound, is able to fill the **whole world** with wonder (v. 3). The next verse shows that the result of the beast's work is to recruit worship both for the dragon and for himself.

Note John's careful use of contrasts to make his point. In an effort to tell this story of good versus evil, John artfully created a contrast between the living God and what some scholars refer to as an unholy trinity made up of the dragon and the two beasts. In John's story, the evil characters are parodies of the good ones. The sea beast can be seen as a kind of antichrist figure. He has **ten crowns on his horns** (v. 1) just as Christ is described as having many crowns (19:12). His heads carry **blasphemous** names (13:1) just as Christ's has a holy name (19:11). And, in the most striking comparison, he is described as having **a fatal wound** (13:3). The Greek word used here is *esphagmene*, and it is used only one more time in this chapter when it describes Christ, **the Lamb that was slain** (v. 8). Additionally, the beast from the earth functions as an unholy spirit. It performs prophetic activity and, as the Holy Spirit has served as an instrument of God's revelation to us, it functions as an instrument of the revelation of evil.

Verse 5 continues the author's work of encouragement by pointing out that while the beast's power is formidable, his time of influence is limited to **forty-two months.** He appears to be winning, but it won't last. The beast fights by attacking God's **name** and by slandering **his dwelling place and those who live in heaven** (v. 6). He makes war on the people of God and is **given authority over every tribe, people, language and nation** (v. 7). By using that phrase—which in other places in Revelation describes the eternal worship given to God—John surely meant to encourage his readers. They knew that the world's worship would ultimately belong to God, and by using those words he was implying the beast's apparent victory is temporary.

Nevertheless, in the short term the beast will be so successful that **all inhabitants of the earth . . . whose names have not been written in the** Lamb's **book of life . . . will worship the beast** (v. 8). This is a key part of this chapter; its placement between the descriptions of the two beasts highlights its importance. John's point was to encourage his audience by reminding them that while most of the world will follow the beast, they who have chosen to receive the grace God has offered them will never find their names taken from the Book of Life by force. The beast's temporary victory, impressive as it is, will not result in their permanent destruction.

WORDS FROM WESLEY

Revelation 13:9

If any man have an ear, let him hear—It was said before, he that hath an ear, let him hear. This expression, *if any*, seems to imply, that scarce will any that hath an ear be found. (ENNT)

Does that mean they'll pass through the beast's rule unscathed? By no means. Verses 9 and 10 seem to say, "Persecuted church, see the situation clearly. Your choice to worship the true God in oppression is the right choice, but it might lead to difficult things." They are reminded that living out the choice to follow God will require **patient endurance and faithfulness** (v. 10).

WORDS FROM WESLEY

Revelation 13:10

If any man leadeth into captivity—God will in due time repay the followers of the beast in their own kind. Meanwhile *here is the patience and faithfulness of the saints*—Exercised: their patience, by enduring captivity or imprisonment; their faithfulness, by resisting unto blood. (ENNT)

The Beast from the Earth (Rev. 13:11–18)

In verse 11 John began to describe a second beast whose nature can be seen in the fact that it **spoke like a dragon.** It goes so far as to perform incredible signs that convince the people of the world to worship the beast, and it then orders them to set up an image of that beast, which it enables to **speak and cause all who refused to worship the image to be killed** (v. 15).

If we are right in assuming the first beast represents the Roman Empire — and scholars are generally in agreement on that point — this second beast must be someone or some structure that supports the first beast's attempts to win the allegiance of the world. Again, some scholars argue that in his depiction of the second beast John was describing the priests and supporters of the emperor cult who were persecuting the Christian minority.

WORDS FROM WESLEY

Revelation 13:16

It is written, that "those who received not the mark of the beast, either on their foreheads, or in their right hands," either openly or secretly, were not permitted "to buy or sell any more." Now, whatever the mystery contained herein may be, I apprehend the plain mark of the beast is wickedness; inward and outward unholiness; whatever is secretly or openly contrary to justice, mercy, or truth. . . . Therefore, many of those who attend on my ministry are, by this means, poorer than before. They will not receive the mark of the beast, either on their forehead or in their hand; or if they had received it before, they rid themselves of it as soon as possible. Some cannot follow their former way of life at all (as pawnbrokers, smugglers, buyers or sellers of uncustomed goods) — others cannot follow it as they did before; for they cannot oppress, cheat, or defraud their neighbour; they cannot lie, or say what they do not mean; they must now speak the truth from their heart. On all these accounts, they have less of this world's goods; because they gain less than they did before. (WJW, vol. 8, 126)

The final verses of the chapter add evidence to this argument. Verses 16 and 17 show that all people, **small and great, rich and poor, free and slave** were required **to receive a** special **mark** if they wanted to be able to engage in commerce (v. 16). The Greek word for this mark—*charagma*—is instructive. This referred to the imperial stamp on commercial documents and the impression of the Emperor's head on a coin. This Roman mark could only be given by the Roman Empire, and all who wanted it had to pledge allegiance to that empire above all else.

In essence, this is a test of worship loyalty. A day is coming when a choice will have to be made. Will the church stand firm and resist the pressure to conform to the empire's model of worship, or will it—at great cost—choose to give worship only to God? Will the church worship the beast or continue to worship God and, supported by His grace, find that their names are still written in the Book of Life? Indeed, that is a question we must all ask ourselves. Where does our loyalty lie? Are our names truly written in the Lamb's Book of Life? Chapter 13 suggests that our choices might reveal the answer to that question.

The final verse of this chapter **calls for wisdom** (v. 18). When John invited those with insight to calculate the number of the beast—which is 666—he was referring to the ancient practice of *gematria*, where each letter of the alphabet was assigned a numerical value (for example, a = 1, b = 2, etc.). People used this to assign number values to words. They could then use those numbers to talk openly about private things with less chance of being understood.

While there are many different theories on the meaning of the number 666, the most widely regarded theory holds that it references the name "Nero." In this case, Nero—the emperor under whom the first and bloodiest persecutions against the church broke out—should perhaps be seen as representative of all the evil aspects of the Roman Empire that were pressuring the church. John included that number, which we assume his audience would have understood, as a way of removing any doubt from his readers' minds—the empire wanted their worship, and they must choose to follow either God or Rome. Middle ground is not an option. It is our choice, today, as well.

DISCUSSION

As a believer, your name is written in the Lamb's Book of Life. Rejoice in that fact today.

1. Do you believe that the beasts are a symbol of evil or real people?

2. What warning do you think this narrative would have offered to those living at the time it was written?

3. What warning does it offer today?

4. What or who are some of the "beasts" we are facing in our world today?

5. What are some of the "proud words and blasphemies" (Rev. 13:5) they utter?

6. By what means do such people or groups rise to "authority over every tribe, people, language and nation" (v. 7)?

7. Why would anyone worship such beasts?

8. Can you name examples of people who were deceived by such "beasts"?

9. How can the church prepare its people to discern any beasts and to resist taking its mark?

PRAYER

God, Creator and Sustainer of the universe, we come before You today to acknowledge You are a mighty God and will win against all Your opponents. Through Your grace we ask that You would sustain us when we face the seductive temptations to give greater loyalty and devotion to our state than to You. Nations, states, and political parties will all pass away, but only You, O God, will last forever.

9

THE REDEEMED FOLLOW THE LAMB

Revelation 14:1–13

Jesus Christ leads His church safely to the end.

Who is the Antichrist? What is the mark of the beast and how will it be used? Who is the Beast? When does the millennium begin? How can you calculate the number of a name? Questions like these have puzzled theologians, futurists, and Bible scholars for hundreds of years. Dozens of answers have been proposed, each with more certainty than the last, only to be disproven or outmoded by more recent experts.

Can we know with certainty who the Antichrist is? Should we try to determine when the end will come? While these questions may have value, endless speculation about them is pointless and counterproductive. The greater purpose of Revelation is to point us toward Christ, whose name we already know and in whom we can have complete confidence.

Chapter 13 of Revelation ended with John's description of the mark that the ruler of earth, the Beast, required everyone to have in order to buy or sell. The name or the number was on each person's hand or forehead. Now the contrast! This study is focused on the Lamb and His followers glorifying and praising their Redeemer. As you dig deeper into the Word of God, you will come to better know the Living Word and have greater confidence in His ability to save and keep you.

COMMENTARY

Revelation offers believers a glimpse of God's perspective—God's eternal victory. Sometimes this perspective is brilliantly clear, and other times it's far from it. Literature of this type is intended to tell the reader there is an unseen perspective (God's) for which the believer must have faith.

This passage seems to be a parenthetical note interrupting a series of judgments. It interrupts to show how the people of God will be protected from God's acts of judgment. In the middle of a series of visions about judgment, believers receive encouragement.

Most anyone interested in the Bible would recognize the twelve tribes of Israel from the Old Testament. But as we look at these tribes, we notice some peculiar things about them. First, they are not in the order they are usually presented in the Old Testament. (See Gen. 29–30; 49:2–27; 1 Chron. 21:2; Ezek. 48:30–34.) Second, Dan is left off the list. Third, Ephraim and Manasseh take the place of Joseph. All these anomalies hint that this listing of the tribes of Israel should not be taken literally.

However, the 144,000 (Rev. 14:1, 3; 7:4–8) and the description of the "unnumbered multitude" (7:9) "before the throne" (14:3; 7:9, 11, 15) are the same group. Several points of similarity support this position. In Revelation 7, from God's vantage point, the 144,000 "from all the tribes of Israel" (7:4) are not only precisely numbered, but also named (7:5–8). However, later in the narrative, from John's perspective, the *human* vantage point, those "standing before the throne" in praise to God are beyond numbering and are not named at all. Those from "every nation, tribe, people and language" (7:9) are the 144,000 "from the earth" (14:3), and the description is repeated in 14:6. Even in Revelation, what humans can only generally observe, God knows in intimate detail: He numbers and names His own.

God Protects His Faithful People (Rev. 14:1–5)

The central focus in this passage again is the Lamb. When we are introduced to the Lamb (ch. 5) the imagery of Christ is clear. The Lamb is standing as if it had been slaughtered, clearly the focus of praise, and the only One worthy to open the scroll of judgment. Here the **Lamb** is **standing on Mount Zion** (14:1). Although **Mount Zion** is only mentioned this one time in Revelation, it is a clear reference to the heavenly Mount Zion described in Hebrews 12:22. Mount Zion is the ancient name for pre-Israelite Jerusalem, captured by David from the Jebusites. It became synonymous as a place of God's presence and future blessing.

WORDS FROM WESLEY

Revelation 14:1

They are now in safety, and have the name of *the Lamb and of his Father written on their foreheads*, as being the redeemed of God and of the Lamb, His now unalienable property. This prophecy often introduces the inhabitants of heaven as a kind of chorus with great propriety and elegance. The church above making suitable reflections on the grand events, which are foretold in this book, greatly serves to raise the attention of real Christians, and to teach the high concern they have in them. Thus is the church on earth instructed, animated, and encouraged, by the sentiments, temper, and devotion of the church in heaven. (ENNT)

In this peaceful interlude, in company with **the Lamb** in the place of blessing are the **144,000**, a symbolic number representing completeness, all faithful believers, **who had his name and his Father's name written on their foreheads** (v. 1). This description matches and elaborates the 144,000 in 7:3 whose foreheads are marked with a seal by God's angels, protecting them from the destructive judgment. This marking coincides with those conquerors in Philadelphia (3:12) who are marked with God's name, and in 22:4 where His people "will see his face, and his name will be on their foreheads." These stand in stark contrast to those who are marked as slaves to the beast in 13:16–17.

Not only is the Lamb present among the 144,000 but He speaks. John described the **sound from heaven** (v. 2) in multiple ways as he did elsewhere in Revelation: **like the roar of rushing waters** (14:2; see 1:15; 19:6), **like a loud peal of thunder** (14:2; see 6:1; 19:6), and yet **like that of harpists playing their harps** (14:2; see 5:8; 15:2).

The large company, identified with the number 144,000 that represents God's accounting, **sang a new song before the throne and before the four living creatures and the elders** (14:3). This new song is one only the **144,000 who had been redeemed** could sing (v. 3). Their song of praise is directed toward the Lamb in response to the melodic and powerful voice they have heard. John further described them as **those who did not defile themselves with women** (v. 4), in comparison to those who defiled themselves with pagan cults, "following after Jezebel" (2:20–22). Perhaps John was continuing the image of the 144,000 as an Old Testament army that called its soldiers to ritual cleanness, which includes sexual matters. (See Deut. 23:9–10; 1 Sam. 21:5; 2 Sam. 11:8–11.)

Wholehearted devotion guides an army to sure and swift victory. Those who **follow the Lamb wherever he goes** (Rev. 14:4) are a reflection of His purity. They, like Him, are **blameless** and **no lie** is **found in their mouths** (v. 5).

God Punishes Those Who Reject Him (Rev. 14:6–11)

After John again presented his readers with the picture of the faithful in the throne room, he moved his perspective in terms of both time and location. In this passage, John offered another presentation of God's faithfulness to present His gospel and to judge those who reject Him.

It seems Revelation is meant to be not a chronological account of transpiring events, but multiple pictures and perspectives of many of the same ideas and events. Recurring or similar words, phrases, descriptions, locations, and announcements tip us off to this. Here in chapter 14 John revisited an idea previously presented, rather than telling us the next chronological happening. Sometimes it might be as simple as giving the reader the picture from a heavenly perspective, and then again from a human perspective.

John refocused his readers' attention away from those who are faithful toward an **angel** proclaiming the **eternal gospel** to **those who live on the earth—to every nation, tribe, language and people** (v. 6). They are urged to **fear God and give him glory** (v. 7). Hardly before the angel is finished with his invitation to **worship** the Creator, the **hour of his judgment is come** (v. 7).

WORDS FROM WESLEY

Revelation 14:7

Fear God and give glory to him; for the hour of his judgment is come—The joyful message is properly this, that the hour of God's judgment is come. And hence is that admonition drawn, *Fear God and give glory to him;* they who do this will not worship the beast, neither any image or idol whatsoever, *and worship him that made*—Whereby He is absolutely distinguished from idols of every kind, *the heaven, and the earth, and the sea, and fountains of water*—And they who worship Him shall be delivered, when the angels pour out their phials on the earth, sea, fountains of water, on the sun, and in the air. (ENNT)

Before anyone responds, John moved the reader to the second angelic announcement. This time the announcement is not an invitation, but rather a pronouncement of judgment on **Babylon the**

Great (v. 8). This is the first of several statements made against Babylon in Revelation. (See 16:19; 17:5; 18:2, 10, 21.) This announcement—**Fallen is Babylon** (14:8)—comes before a complete description of Babylon fallen is offered in chapter 18, another example of events in Revelation not following chronological order.

Scholars' interpretations vary widely regarding Babylon the Great—from an image of political power and wealth and decadence to a reference to the world empire of Mesopotamian history. Condemnation of historic Babylon is found in the Old Testament (see Isa. 21:9; Jer. 51:8), but Peter's reference to Babylon couldn't refer to the historical Babylon. (See 1 Pet. 5:13.) Throughout church history, the New Testament allusion to Babylon shared by Peter and John has been thought to refer primarily to Rome but applied to any seductive, economically powerful entity. Often scholars adjust their interpretations to refer to current political and economic powerhouses. Godless Babylon is indicted because it has coerced all nations to align themselves with it, or as John poetically stated it, to **drink the maddening wine of her adulteries** (Rev. 14:8). Certainly, the lure of monetary benefit has made for strange bedfellows, whether between individuals or nations.

WORDS FROM WESLEY
Revelation 14:10

He shall drink—With Babylon (ch. 16:19), *and shall be tormented*—With the beast (ch. 20:10). In all the Scripture there is not another so terrible threatening as this. And God by this greater fear arms His servants against tine fear of the beast. *The wrath of God which is poured unmixed*—Without any mixture of mercy, without hope, *into the cup of his indignation*—And it no real anger implied in all this? O what will not even wise men assert, to serve an hypothesis! (ENNT)

Yet **a third angel** appears announcing judgment on **anyone who worships the beast and his image and receives his mark on the forehead or on the hand** (v. 9). In the same way as they drank the wine of Babylon's adulteries, here they are forced to **drink of the wine of God's fury** (v. 10). This fury, instead of being diluted, as is common with wine, is a **full strength** portion of God's **wrath** (v. 10). John continued a horrific description of God's punishment for **those who worship the beast and his image, or for anyone who receives the mark of his name** (v. 11). Like Sodom and Gomorrah (Gen. 19:24) and the wicked of Psalm 11:6, they **will be tormented with burning sulfur** (Rev. 14:10), a noxious, suffocating gas. It is an ongoing, **for ever and ever** (v. 11), burning pain administered **in the presence of the holy angels and of the Lamb** (v. 10). No mention is made of those who follow the Lamb. Those who are protected by God's mark apparently are also protected from witnessing this horrible judgment.

Call for Endurance (Rev. 14:12–13)

The contrast of those who are worshiping in the presence of the throne (14:1–5) and those who are suffering God's punishment (14:6–11) is stark. Yet after the terrible picture of God's wrath, John's readers were called back to the comfort of God's presence. John urged the **saints** to **patient endurance**, to **obey God's commandments and remain faithful to Jesus** (v. 12).

Upon God's command to **write** (v. 13), John presented the second of seven blessings (beatitudes) in Revelation (1:3; 16:15; 19:9; 20:6; 22:7, 14). **Blessed** (14:13) means "in a gracious position" or "to be congratulated, because of God's obvious favoring." The word *happy* doesn't even begin to describe the depth of this good standing.

WORDS FROM WESLEY
Revelation 14:13

And I heard a voice—This is most seasonably heard, when the beast is in his highest power and fury, *out of heaven*—Probably from a departed saint, *Write*—He was at first commanded to write the whole book. Whenever this is repeated, it denotes something peculiarly observable. *Happy are the dead (from henceforth* particularly)—1. Because they escape the approaching calamities; 2. Because they already enjoy so near an approach to glory; *who die in the Lord*—In the faith of the Lord Jesus, *for they rest*—No pain, no purgatory follows; but pure, unmixed happiness, *from their labours*—And the more laborious their life was, the sweeter is their rest. How different this state from that of those (ver. 11), *who have no rest day or night*? Reader, which wilt thou choose? *Their works*—Each one's peculiar works, *follow*—Or accompany them: that is, the fruit of their works. Their works do not go before, to procure them admittance into the mansions of joy; but they follow them when admitted. (ENNT)

It is ironic to read **blessed are the dead** (v. 13). The reader is compelled to read on to get an explanation of why one who is dead is in such good standing. The explanation is forthcoming: Those **who die in the Lord . . . will rest from their labor** (v. 13). This promise stands in absolute contrast to the punishment of "those who worship the beast" for whom "there is no rest day or night" (v. 11). In the same way the faithful "follow the Lamb wherever he goes" (v. 4), the **deeds** of those who endure, who die in the Lord, **will follow them**, and they will rest from their labor (v. 13).

DISCUSSION

Reflect on how the book of Revelation scares, thrills, or affects you.

1. How does this study's passage differ from the previous one?

2. Bible scholars can't agree about whether the number of those saved presented here is a literal or symbolic figure. Either way, who are those who will be included?

3. What do you think is meant by having the Lamb's name and His Father's name written on the forehead?

4. What do you think is meant by "those who did not defile themselves . . . for they kept themselves pure" (Rev. 14:4)?

5. What do you think is meant by "they follow the Lamb wherever he goes" (v. 4)?

6. How closely does the church today resemble these 144,000? What similarities or differences can you name?

7. How closely do you resemble those characteristics?

8. What is patient endurance? Why do you think this would be important for Christians? Do you possess patient endurance?

9. What advice would you give to your Christian friends based on this study?

PRAYER

Dear Lord, our heavenly Father, You are faithful to us even when times are tough and it appears Your enemies are gaining the upper hand. Please give us strength to believe that Your enemies will not prevail, but You will reign supreme forever.

10

POWER, GREED, AND FAITH

Revelation 17:1–18

Christ, the Lamb will be victorious.

Given the all-too-real effects of evil in our world—including poverty, hunger, genocide, and abortion—it would be tempting to believe that these evil megalomaniacs have been successful. We might be tempted to withdraw from the world, believing it is entirely corrupt and irredeemable.

But here comes our hero! The Lamb, the grand hero of Revelation, is alive and well, and in the end will vanquish the agents of evil.

This study reminds us that our belief in Jesus Christ is not a comic book fantasy but a reliable hope in a trustworthy and powerful person. We take comfort in the fact that, although the battle may *seem* in doubt, the ending is assured. The Lamb has overcome.

COMMENTARY

Revelation 15 and 16 add to the vision's groups of seven: "seven angels with the seven last plagues" (15:1). Revelation 16:1 renames the "plagues" as "the seven bowls of God's wrath." One of the wrath-related angels opens the unit in chapter 17 of the ongoing vision.

You may wish to compare this chapter's woman and beast (allies) with the woman and beast of Revelation 12. In the earlier chapter, the woman and beast are opposed, with the woman (representing Mary) bearing a son that the beast seeks to devour.

And 12:5 describes the "male child" ruling "all the nations with an iron scepter." This parallels the portrayal in 17:14 of the Lamb as "Lord of lords and King of kings."

The Woman (Rev. 17:1–6, 18)

Revelation 17:5 identifies its woman as **Babylon**. Why Babylon? Babylon had been the capital of the Babylonian Empire, the center that destroyed Jerusalem and carried God's Old Testament people into exile. Babylon had been the great enemy of God's people, the role now carried by Rome, the capital of the empire that had exiled John the apostle and persecuted followers of Jesus Christ. So the woman is a symbol for Babylon, which itself symbolizes the reality of which John spoke—Rome.

WORDS FROM WESLEY

Revelation 17:5

Yea, what is most dreadful, most to be lamented of all, these Christian churches . . . that bear the name of Christ, the Prince of Peace, and wage continual war with each other! that convert sinners by burning them alive! that are "drunk with the blood of the saints!"—Does this praise belong only to "Babylon the Great, the mother of harlots and abominations of the earth?" Nay, verily; . . . Protestant churches too know to persecute, when they have power in their hands, even unto blood. And, meanwhile, how do they also anathematize each other! devote each other to the nethermost hell! What wrath, what contention, what malice, what bitterness, is everywhere found among them, even where they agree in essentials, and only differ in opinions, or in the circumstantials of religion! Who follows after *only* the "things that make for peace, and things wherewith one may edify another?" O God! how long? Shall thy promise fail? Fear it not, ye little flock! Against hope, believe in hope! It is your Father's good pleasure yet to renew the face of the earth. Surely all these things shall come to an end, and the inhabitants of the earth shall learn righteousness. (WJW, vol. 5, 277)

The woman is described as sitting on a **beast** (v. 3), **many waters** (v. 1), and **seven hills** (v. 9). The waters are associated with Babylon, one in the multiple layers of symbolism. Jeremiah 51:13 portrays the ancient city as living "by many waters." Rome is surrounded by seven hills. Many writers of the Roman Empire, including Virgil and Cicero, joined John in describing Rome as the city of seven hills. (For further confirmation that the woman represented Rome, see Rev. 17:18.)

Within his vision, John saw the woman **dressed in purple and scarlet, . . . glittering with gold, precious stones and pearls** (v. 4). This imagery portrays the luxury of the Roman emperor and his elite comrades.

John's vision left no doubt as to the wealthy woman's character. The angel identified her as a **prostitute** (v. 1). Within ancient Jewish-Christian culture, prostitution was as low as a woman could go into the depths of evil. Roman prostitutes wore head gear with labels hanging down over their foreheads. This woman's label identified her not only as a prostitute, but as **the mother of prostitutes** (v. 5). John saw Rome not only as evil, but as the queen of evil.

WORDS FROM WESLEY

Revelation 17:6

And I saw the woman drunk with the blood of the saints—So that Rome may well be called, *The slaughter-house of the martyrs*. She hath shed much Christian blood in every age; but at length she is even drunk with it, at the time to which this vision refers. *The witnesses of Jesus*—The preachers of His word; *And I wondered exceedingly*—At her cruelty and the patience of God. (ENNT)

Within John's vision, what made the woman and the empire she represented so dark? **She held a golden cup in her hand, filled with abominable things** (v. 4). The contents of this cup made her

drunk (v. 6). What were those contents? **The blood of those who bore testimony to Jesus** (v. 6). These latter verses describe Babylon drinking from, and offering to others, a cup of evil. Rome not only killed those who saw Jesus (rather than Caesar) as Lord. It gloried in their deaths as a drunken person revels in liquor.

The Beast (Rev. 17:7–13)

If the woman of evil is Rome, the beast seems to represent several entities who associate with her. The beast is "covered with blasphemous names" (17:3). These names might indicate Rome's many idols, the false gods whose temples covered the city's hillsides. Or the words written on the sides of the beast may stand for the honorific titles Rome's emperors bore, titles that should be reserved for God alone: Revered One, Divine One, Savior, and Lord.

Puzzlingly, the beast is later described as a being who **once was, now is not, and will come up** again (v. 8). What does this mean? Some speculate the detail in the vision indicated Nero, an evil emperor from about thirty years before John's writing, had been killed, but legend indicated he had risen again, was now in hiding, and would return to retake his throne. In any case, John intended his readers to see the beast as a representation of evil, who (both in their history and throughout history) sometimes appears to be conquered at least momentarily, but inevitably returns in greater power.

The beast has **seven heads** (vv. 3, 9; compare 13:1). From one perspective, these heads are the **hills** of Rome (17:9). So in some sense, both the woman and the beast on which she sits are to be identified as Rome and its rulers. From yet another perspective, the beast's seven heads represent **seven kings, five** of whom **have fallen, one is,** and another who **has not yet come** (v. 10). What is the meaning to this puzzle? We can't be sure, but some speculate the beast's first five heads indicated Rome's first five emperors: Caesar Augustus, Tiberius, Caligula, Claudius, and Nero. If this is true, then the one who is might be Vespasian. The seventh who would **remain** but **a little while** would be Titus (v. 10; Titus reigned only two years). The **eighth king** of 17:11? That would be Domitian, the evil emperor who was the first to require that he be worshiped as a god, the one who had exiled John and broadly persecuted the Christian church.

WORDS FROM WESLEY

Revelation 17:8

O how great is that darkness! It is the very smoke which ascends out of the bottomless pit! It is the essential night which reigns in the lowest deep, in the land of the shadow of death! (WJW, vol. 5, 365)

The identity of the woman as Rome is certain. The interpretation of the beast, its heads and horns we can hold more tentatively. To complicate our work, the beast had seven heads representing seven kings (followed by an eighth) and **ten horns** representing **ten kings** (v. 12). If the seven heads are seven (plus one) emperors, then who are the ten kings? Here we return to a foundational premise in interpreting Revelation: Neither God nor John may have intended John's original (and twenty-first-century) readers to gain a precise meaning for every detail in the extended vision. Perhaps all the beast's heads and horns, as well as the complete picture of the beast itself, represent evil in all its manifestations—then, since, and now. Perhaps the woman did represent first-century Rome, as well as all subsequent governments that line themselves up against God and His people.

The Angel (Rev. 17:1, 3, 7)

Throughout Revelation, God uses angels as the bearers of His message-carrying vision. (See, for example, 5:2; 7:2; 8:2; 10:1; 14:6, 8, 9; 15:1.) The angel of 17:1 is one of the **seven** described in 15:1.

John (Rev. 17:3, 6)

The **angel** who spoke to John, introducing this segment of the vision, **carried** him **away** (v. 3). Did John move only in his mind, or was he physically carried? We cannot be sure. John indicated that the **angel carried** him **in the Spirit** (v. 3). John would see the representations of evil, but only from the security of God's protecting presence (compare 1:10). To what location was John carried? A **desert**, the wilderness, in ancient times the place beyond the safety of population centers, a place where evil lurked. (Compare Jesus being tempted in the desert [Matt. 4:1–11].)

When John shuddered at the sight of the woman and beast, the angel did not leave John in fear of her attack, but gave him the full story of the Lamb who would overcome her, bringing John and other disciples victory.

The Lamb (Rev. 17:14)

No matter how interpreters view the rest of this chapter, its meaning revolves around 17:14, its core: **They will make war against the Lamb, but the Lamb will overcome them because he is Lord of lords and King of kings—and with him will be his called, chosen and faithful followers.**

A great battle would be waged. (In the first century, the end of time, or across the centuries? Probably all three.) Who would be the combatants? On one side, the forces of evil, in this chapter represented by the evil woman (Rome and all its successor God-forsaking governments) and the beast (all forces of evil used by evil people in power). On the other side, the Lamb. The lamb obviously represents vulnerability. More specifically, throughout Scripture (and earlier in Revelation), a lamb symbolizes the One who gave himself as a sacrifice for the world (Isa. 53:7; John 1:29; 1 Pet. 1:19; Rev. 5:6; 13:8). But although this Lamb had made himself vulnerable, even offering himself to death, He had moved out of weakness into a position of victory.

The Lamb will overcome the evil woman and beast, all the forces of evil **because he is Lord of lords and King of kings** (17:14). Even if the woman is Rome (the greatest military force the world had yet seen) and the beast represents its emperors (the most powerful individuals in history to that point), the forces of evil had met their match and more in the One more powerful than any other supposed lord, any other king. Again, we can ask if the Lamb's victory should be seen as an event in the first century, the end of time, or all of history. Again, we answer—all three. Individual Christians might suffer and die, but the church and its King would survive all evil emperors, then and now. And in the end, evil will be banished from God's eternal kingdom.

WORDS FROM WESLEY

Revelation 17:14

These—Kings with the beast. *Shall make war with the Lamb. He is Lord of lords*—Rightful Sovereign of all, and ruling all things well; *and King of kings*—As a King He fights with, and conquers all His enemies. *And they that are with him*—Beholding His victory, are such as were, while in the body, called by His word and Spirit, *and chosen*—Taken out of the world, when they were enabled to believe in Him, *and faithful*—Unto death. (ENNT)

The residents of that kingdom? Not conquered nations there, outside their hopes and plans (the plight of most people within the Roman Empire). No, citizenship in this kingdom will be the prized possession of Jesus' **called, chosen and faithful followers** (v. 14). First-century legend might have Nero returning to life. But a fact of all centuries is the resurrection to new and eternal life of those whom Nero and other evil rulers have killed (6:9–11), the ones whose blood the evil woman gloried in drinking (17:6). Those who have followed Jesus will reign with Him.

The Epilogue (Rev. 17:15–17)

If the Lamb and His followers reign forever, what happens to the forces of evil? Within the imagery of vision, they destroy each other. **The beast and the ten horns you saw will hate the prostitute. They will bring her to ruin and leave her naked; they will eat her flesh and burn her with fire** (v. 16). Good recognizes and cooperates with good. Evil may partner with evil for a time, but evil entities, in time, desire ultimate rule and following their nature, competing against each other even to death. God knows this. In line with 17:17, God allows evil forces to exert power for a time, until He is ready to defeat them or lead them to defeat one another.

Who is left in this story? The **peoples, multitudes, nations and languages** (v. 15) who may find themselves currently under the rule of evil. Within the vision, these people groups are seen as the **waters . . . where the prostitute sits** (v. 15). To them, choice is given. They can, for benefit in the short run, identify themselves with the evil of this world. Or, for their eternal benefit, they can hear the call of Jesus to become His faithful followers (17:17). They can enjoy favor now or reign with the Ultimate Victor forever.

*Portions of this commentary lean on William Barclay, *The Revelation of John* (Philadelphia: Westminster Press, 1960), 2:175–186.

DISCUSSION

Reflect on when you let power and greed overcome you. Now repent.

1. What is it about marriage that is so precious to God? And why is unfaithfulness in marriage so offensive to God?

2. What or who do you think "the great prostitute" (Rev. 17:1) represents?

3. The text says that "the inhabitants of the earth were intoxicated with the wine of her adulteries" (v. 2). What clues do we have of what makes her so attractive?

4. In what ways do you see the unholy trinity of money, sex, and power exercising influence in the world today? Do you see any of these effects in the church as well?

5. What do you think is the significance of having the word *Babylon* written on her forehead?

6. What could it mean that this woman is "drunk with the blood of the saints" (v. 6)?

7. What false religions do you see in the world today? What is their effect upon the world?

8. What political powers today are warring against Christ's church?

9. Whose purposes is this adulteress accomplishing? God's? The world's? The Enemy's?

10. How can the church today safeguard itself from being lured into the trap described in this passage?

11. What hope does God providence to accomplish his purpose give to those going through persecution?

PRAYER

God, we confess that we tend to rely on fleshly power in our battle against evil. Bring us back to Your instruction on pulling down evil's strongholds by bringing us back to our knees in prayer.

CELEBRATE THE LAMB

Revelation 19:1–10

In worship, we celebrate God's victories—past and future.

This study gives us a glimpse of the celebration that will take place in heaven when all the saints of the ages finally join together, giving thanks that all earthly temptations and persecutions are forever done. Praise also rises for the long-awaited full reign of God and the wedding of the Lamb. Until then, our earthly celebration in worship is practice for the grand celebration we will see there.

While the vision revealed here astonished even John when he witnessed it, this portion of Scripture gives us an inkling of the celebration we can expect in heaven. Perhaps too complex and wonderful to be fully understood now, these verses will at least whet our appetite for the joy that is in store for us.

COMMENTARY

This chapter is a conclusion to the drama that began in chapter 17 and continued through chapter 18. It is also a transition from the preceding drama of judgments and catastrophic events to celebration of victory and final establishment of God's kingdom. With this chapter the tone of the book shifts. It is one of great celebration and worship, opening us to explore many dimensions of worship.

The twenty-four elders and four living creatures introduced in chapter 4 play a central role in moving events along. While they have been present throughout Revelation, at this point they move to the forefront. They act as a worship team, demonstrating uninhibited, authentic worship.

A survey of this passage gives rise to a few observations. First, the visual layout reveals a poetic flow. The verses naturally divide into four sections, each beginning with "Hallelujah." Second, there are two divisions within these four sections, each containing two couplets. Third, we notice many words of adoration and exaltation, to remind us we can anticipate a passage of great worship. The two larger divisions exemplify praise for the destruction of God's enemy and praise for the victory of God's kingdom.

Praise for the Destruction of God's Enemy (Rev. 19:1–3)

Chapter 17 introduced the great prostitute who dominates through chapter 18. It is obvious that this character is an enemy of God, seeking to destroy the kingdom of God. One of the promises and words of hope that has prevailed in this book is that the enemies of God would be judged and defeated. This defeat took place in the previous chapter, and now the celebration begins.

John described the celebration: **I heard what sounded like the roar of a great multitude in heaven shouting** (v. 1). The use of sensory stimulation is incredible. Visualize a vast crowd as far as the eye can see in every direction. In one voice, they cry out in praise. The noise so deafening, children cover their ears. Unlike the roar of many crowds, the unison allows the writer to understand precisely what is being said.

They shout, **"Hallelujah"** (v. 1), a word comprised of two Hebrew words—*halal* and *jah*—meaning "praise Yahweh." In more contemporary terms, "Praise the Lord!" The term *halal* refers to a series of psalms used in the celebration of Passover as pilgrims made their way to the temple. It is appropriate that such a term would be part of such a word of exaltation. This is the only place in the New Testament where this word is found.

The praise of the multitude is rooted in the victory of God over the great prostitute. The accolades attributed to God are like those given to victorious kings of battle. The word **salvation** used in verse 1 denotes God's salvation from the enemy, the great prostitute. We often forget that with victory comes the possibility of defeat. Therefore, the celebration is authentic, not fabricated.

WORDS FROM WESLEY

Revelation 19:1

I heard a loud voice of a great multitude—Whose blood the great whore had shed, *saying, Hallelujah*—This Hebrew word signifies, Praise ye Jah, or Him that is. (ENNT)

Further accolades are based on the balanced discernment of God. It is said of Him, **true and just are his judgments** (v. 2). His decisions are untainted by prejudice or bribery. His only concern is the welfare of His children and kingdom. All enemies of the kingdom of God can expect demise. The judgment and condemnation of the great prostitute is due to her attempt to defeat the kingdom of God by corrupting God's people. This condemnation is complete and final.

In chapter 6, we were allowed to glimpse a group huddled under the altar who had been martyred for their testimony of Jesus. They cried out to God, asking how long it would be before their blood was avenged (see Rev. 6:9–11). This concept alludes to the Levitical law requiring the kinsman-redeemer to avenge the blood of a murder victim. Here in chapter 19, we have another allusion to this avenging: **He has avenged on her the blood of his servants** (19:2). There is a sense of repressed anger and judgment being released upon the prostitute resulting in annihilation.

Between verses 2 and 3 there may have been a pause of consideration as verse 3 begins with the multitude again shouting. Perhaps the concept of God's servants being avenged caused the multitude to pause in a moment of silence for these great examples of faith. Further, the realization that this great defeat of the prostitute, the enemy of God, held such significance would cause reflective silence. Its implications are magnanimous.

This second section of praise is like an encore of exaltation. It is based on the finality of the destruction of the prostitute. **The smoke from her goes up for ever and ever** (v. 3). This phrase should not be taken too literally, and probably means that this act is final and will be known forever. This is a clear and unmistakable message to any and all enemies of God as to their final destiny.

This brings the first division of this poem of praise to an end. It reminds us of our security in the kingdom of God; all enemies of God will be defeated. It reveals Jesus Christ, and His ministry as the inauguration of a victorious kingdom.

Praise for the Victory of God's Kingdom (Rev. 19:4–8)

The twenty-four elders and the four living creatures, acting as narrators moving the action along, respond to the great encore of the first division of this passage. Their response duplicates the doxology of Psalm 106, a *Hallel* psalm, with the words, **"Amen, Hallelujah!"** (Rev. 19:4). This seems to stimulate a call to praise God that encompasses **all you his servants, you who fear him, both small and great!** (v. 5).

The response to the call to praise is astounding. The description in verse 6 of the sound of this response is intended to demonstrate that this event is even greater than that of verse 1. John equated the sound with **the roar of rushing waters and like loud peals of thunder** (v. 6). One gets the sense that John was grasping for adequate descriptors. The decibel level of this event must have been unequaled in history. This indicates the vast number of worshipers of God and the intensity of their expressions of praise. These expressions of praise lift us to a higher level of exaltation of God in this second section of the second division of this poem of praise.

The praise of the multitude is rooted in the victory of God's kingdom. As important as the defeat of the enemy of God is the final establishment of His kingdom. Many kingdoms have defeated their enemies but have not been able to maintain their victorious reign. This is not the case with God and His kingdom. This anthem of praise begins, **"Hallelujah! For our Lord God Almighty reigns"** (v. 6). This exaltation exhibits great confidence on behalf of John, who was writing during the powerful reign of the Roman Empire. Several emperors had declared they were Lord and God. John added the term **Almighty** to distinguish our God as superior to all. At the same time, **our** establishes that God is personal. What an incredible thought that often escapes us: the almighty God, ruler of the universe, is personal to us as well.

The call to **rejoice and be glad** (v. 7) echoes the words of Jesus in Matthew 5:12 and describes our response to persecution because of the reward awaiting us. Now this reward is revealed: the great wedding feast of Jesus and His bride. Regardless of the view one accepts, this marriage of the Lamb depicts the union of Jesus with His church and is a source of great rejoicing for us even now.

WORDS FROM WESLEY

Revelation 19:6

Sing with glad anticipation,
Mortals and immortals sing,
Jesus comes with full salvation,
Jesus doth His glory bring,
Hallelujah,
God omnipotent is King! (PW, vol. 13, 238)

The language of God's relationship with His people being equated with marriage is found throughout the prophetic literature, the Gospels, and the writings of Paul. The traditional wedding of biblical times involved two parts. First was the betrothal, separated in time from the second part, the actual wedding. One was referred to as *spouse* from betrothal forward. This was a time of anticipation and preparation for the climactic event of the wedding. This is analogous to the church, betrothed and waiting for the final appearance of Jesus for the wedding event. This is a tender picture of our situation and further establishes the state of victory enjoyed by the overcoming Lamb of God in the victorious kingdom of God.

The adornment of the bride is **fine linen, bright and clean** (Rev. 19:8). This is in contrast to the prostitute who was adorned "in purple and scarlet, and was glittering with gold, precious stones and pearls" (17:4). The **fine linen stands for the righteous acts of the saints** (19:8). Our proper response to the saving grace of God is a life of holiness, evidenced by righteous acts. We were created for good works although we are saved by faith through God's grace.

WORDS FROM WESLEY

Revelation 19:8

And it is given to her—By God—The bride is, all holy men, the whole invisible church, *to be arrayed in fine linen, white and clean*—This is an emblem of *the righteousness of the saints*—Both of their justification and sanctification. (ENNT)

With this parenthetic phrase, this great anthem of praise comes to a conclusion. It blends many pictures from both the Old and New Testaments, leaving us with a feeling of awe. In describing an indescribable scene, John wove together these pictures that challenge us to rejoice in our victorious God and worship Him in His basic attributes.

Explanation for the Worship of God (Rev. 19:9–10)

John was given instructions by the angel to write. One wonders if John was so caught up in the display before him that he forgot his mission to write down what he saw. The angel specifically told him to **write: "Blessed are those who are invited to the wedding supper of the Lamb!"** (v. 9). This is the fourth beatitude of Revelation. The idea of a sacred meal of the Messiah with His people is common in Jewish thought. Jesus referenced this event during the Last Supper when He instituted the sacrament of the Lord's Supper (Matt. 26:29). What a promise to those hearing this message for the first time during intense persecution. What hope inspired by the fact that this promise was not forgotten. The assurance that they were "blessed" would bring a glimmer of that joy now.

Caught up in the moment of worship, it appears John mistook the angel for the Lord himself as he fell down in worship. The angel admonished him not to do this, because he was simply a servant like John. He then commanded, **Worship God!** (Rev. 19:10). Only God is worthy of worship and praise. No matter how grateful we may be to the one who brings the message, our worship is reserved for God. This worship is attested by Jesus and is the essence of the prophetic proclamation.

WORDS FROM WESLEY
Revelation 19:10

And I fell before his feet to worship him—It seems, mistaking him for the Angel of the covenant, *but he saith, See thou do it not*—In the original, it is only See not, with a beautiful abruptness. To pray to, or worship the highest creature, is flat idolatry. *I am thy fellow-servant, and of thy brethren that have the testimony of Jesus*—I am now employed as your fellow-servant to testify of the Lord Jesus, by the same Spirit which inspired the prophets of old. (ENNT)

In this passage the curtain has opened, allowing us to view this great act playing out in heaven. It reveals the final establishment of the kingdom inaugurated by Jesus through His ministry. We find great cause for rejoicing with the myriad of believers throughout history depicted here. In one great multitude, we lift our voices in praise for the destruction of God's enemies and for the victory of God's kingdom. We further rejoice with the saints of all time that we are counted with the "blessed" who are invited to the wedding supper of the Lamb. Our hope is secured by the words of the angel to John: **These are the true words of God** (v. 9). Hallelujah, amen!

DISCUSSION

One reason the book of Revelation was written was to be an encouragement for Christians going through intense persecution.

1. How does Revelation 19:1–2 encourage us as we go through difficult personal or political times?

2. How can we keep encouraged when justice seems delayed?

3. According to verse 5, what should be our emotional response as come before God is worship? How has the church lost that awe and "fear" in our worship?

4. Throughout Scripture, marriage is used as a symbol of the joyful, intimate relationship of God and His people. How is this image portrayed in this study?

5. The bride was given "linen, bright and clean" to wear which "stands for the righteous acts of the saint" (v. 8). How are we "given" righteousness?

6. How well has the church done as preparing itself for the groom's return? In what ways could it do better?

7. How does Christ's parable of the wise and foolish virgins (Matt. 25) relate to this passage?

PRAYER

God our Father, Jesus Christ the Son, and the precious Holy Spirit, enable us to approach You in worship with the attitude of those who worship You continually at Your throne in heaven so we will be prepared to join the great throng on some future day.

12

A NEW HEAVEN AND A NEW EARTH

Revelation 21:1–7, 22–27

Christians look forward to living in the presence of Christ forever.

For every winner, there is a loser. This is true in most areas of life. In the real world, not everyone is a winner. That applies to the spiritual realm as well. At the end of time, when the great contest between Christ and the Beast is finally over, the Lord Jesus Christ will stand as the victor, and His chosen ones will stand with Him. Others will be defeated and will know only regret.

This study reminds us of the prize awaiting those who are victorious. God will create a new heaven and a new earth, in which He makes everything new. The most magnificent part of heaven is that God will be there. He and the Lamb will be its temple and its light. This is a prize worth fighting for.

COMMENTARY

The context of Revelation 21 and 22 is not just the rest of Revelation. Since these chapters are the climax of the Christian Bible, their context is the whole Bible, beginning with Genesis 1 and 2. This is the basis of the observation that God's creation-redemption relationship with the human race began in a garden, the garden of Eden, and ends in a city, the New Jerusalem coming down out of heaven, adorned as a bride for her husband.

The new and holy city is a major focus of Revelation 21. The garden (or at least its focal point), now within the city, is the climax of this portrayal. These two chapters, Revelation 21–22, give our only extended glimpse into the promised future fulfillment, just as Genesis 1–2 give our only extended look at God's original creation intentions.

Another aspect of context for this study is the observation that the cataclysmic upheavals portrayed throughout much of Revelation have ended. The final enemies, death and Hades, have been dismissed forever (20:14). God's original and ultimate intentions no longer reside partially in the realm of the "not yet." Now, all is won; all is finished; all is new; all is joy; all is shalom, God's perfect peace.

God Will Dwell with Them (Rev. 21:1–4)

With all evil removed forever (20:14–15), John's attention was drawn to **a new heaven and a new earth** (21:1). In light of several passages in Isaiah, and Paul's avowal (Rom. 8:18–22) that all creation awaits its final redemption, most New Testament scholars understand John to mean the complete renewal of the heavens and the earth, purged of all evil, cured and cleansed of all its ill effects. John Wesley suggested the perfection of God's restoration will surpass even what would have happened had sin never entered the world.

What did the apostle John mean by the statement, **there was no longer any sea** (Rev. 21:1)? Earlier in Revelation, the sea had been the source of the evil beast that led the whole world to worship the dragon, and himself as well, and which made war against the saints of God (13:1–8). The notice that now, in God's perfectly restored creation, there is no more sea may be a way of saying that all sources of evil have been removed, whatever the "sea" may be, or represent here, in the highly metaphorical language of apocalyptic. We ought to allow for the possibility, too, that John meant this statement more literally, and that the earth, renewed, may be different in important ways than it is now.

That the eternal dwellings of God's people will include the earth is indicated also by John's vision of **the Holy City, the**

new Jerusalem, coming down out of heaven from God (21:2). We usually think of heaven largely in terms of John's description of the city in this chapter and the beginning of the next, and rightly so. But the city is not all there is to heaven. Moreover, the city is not—or will not be—"up there," as we usually think of it. John was clear: He saw the heavenly city coming down upon the earth. Earth, too, will be part of heaven when all is as it should be.

John described the city **as a bride** (v. 2). This is in vivid and intentional contrast with the earlier portrayal of Babylon (Rome and the ungodly systems of the world) generally as the great prostitute (chs. 17–18). As wicked and impure as is that prostitute—no, John intended a much greater contrast—much more is the bride pure and holy.

WORDS FROM WESLEY

Revelation 21:2

And I saw the holy city—The new heaven, the new earth, and the new Jerusalem, are closely connected. This city is wholly new, belonging not to this world, not to the millennium, but to eternity. (ENNT)

We may expect **a loud voice from the throne** (v. 3) to be the voice of God. The declarations that follow are third person, though, not first person. This may suggest, but does not require, another speaker. As humans sometimes do of themselves, God too may speak of himself in the third person.

The first declaration announces the permanent fulfillment of the most important goal of the Old Testament. God's redemption intention from the beginning has been to live in such intimate fellowship with human beings (not with Israel only) that **they will be his people, and God . . . will be . . . their God** (v. 3). In his gospel, John affirmed Jesus' earthly life as the beginning of the fulfillment of this intention (promise), in the phrasing, "The Word became flesh and made his dwelling among us" (John 1:14). "Made his dwelling" is the same Greek root as **the dwelling** and **he will live** (dwell) here in Revelation 21:3. What began in Jesus' earthly lifetime now will continue eternally.

It is true that *dwell* and *dwelling* referred originally, and still may refer, to a tent. However, just as a tent always has been the preferred and permanent dwelling of pastoral nomads of the Middle East and beyond, so this dwelling of God among God's people need not connote temporary abode. The language here is all of permanence, and certainly John's description of the city, following these paragraphs, is not at all tent-like.

Several Greek manuscripts read "they will be His peoples" (not "people"); the standard scholarly edition of the Greek New Testament has adopted this reading. *Peoples* includes the ethnic groups from whom the whole family of God has been and will be drawn. Israel is included in this promise, but so are all the gentile people groups. (Compare Rev. 5:9–10.)

The promise of God personally wiping away tears is repeated from Isaiah 25:8, as is the promise of no more death, though John reversed Isaiah's order. The image of God standing before the believer who has come home for good, wiping the tears from their faces, and perhaps saying at that moment, "Welcome home, children," is enough to bring tears of joy and longing to the eyes of the faithful who dwell this side of John's vision. To dwell eternally with God, to be forever finished with **death** and **mourning** and **crying** and **pain** is a worthy hope, indeed (Rev. 21:4).

"I Am Making Everything New!" (Rev. 21:5–7)

He who was seated on the throne (v. 5) identified himself in verse 6 as **the Alpha and the Omega, the Beginning and the End.** (*Alpha* and *omega* are the first and last letters of the Greek alphabet.) In the next chapter (22:13), Jesus used this title of himself; in other places (for example, 1:8) it may be used of God the Father or, possibly, it may refer there also to Jesus. The point is, what is true here of one person of the Trinity is true of all three persons of the Trinity: each is from the beginning and without end.

What the Speaker seated on the throne says in this paragraph seems to identify Him as Jesus. Jesus' sacrificial death at Calvary, together with His resurrection three days later, is the work that made all things new. Earlier, Jesus told John to write (1:19). Jesus also promised water to the thirsty (John 4:14; 6:35; 7:37–38).

WORDS FROM WESLEY
Revelation 21:5

What a strange scene is here opened to our view! How remote from all our natural apprehensions! Not a glimpse of what is here revealed was ever seen in the heathen world. Not only the modern, barbarous, uncivilized Heathens have not the least conception of it; but it was equally unknown to the refined, polished Heathens of ancient Greece and Rome. And it is almost as little thought of or understood by the generality of Christians: I mean, not barely those that are nominally such; that have the form of godliness without the power; but even those that in a measure fear God, and study to work righteousness. (WJW, vol. 6. 288–289)

Write this down (Rev. 21:5). The Greek here is stronger and more emphatic, a single verb of command: "Write!" Sometimes much is made of the oral nature of ancient cultures. Yet from its beginning, writing has been used to record events so they would be remembered correctly, and to record promises and other contracts as indicators of the good faith of those making them. Jesus, seated on the heavenly throne in John's vision here, did not hesitate to give this same kind of firm assurance that what John had witnessed would come to pass.

It is done (v. 6) is a single Greek verb; its past perfect form is another indication of the strength of the affirmation and assurance of this speech. Though in John's day, and down to our own, we do not yet see it happening, in God's settled purposes it already is done. We may rely on it, because we may rely on God's purpose and on God's Word affirming that purpose.

WORDS FROM WESLEY

Revelation 21:6

That sat upon the throne, *said to me, It is done* — All that the prophets had spoken, all that was spoken ch. 4:1. We read this expression twice in this prophecy: first (ch. 16:17) at the fulfilling of the wrath of God, and here at the making all things new. (ENNT)

The promise of **drink without cost** (v. 6) marks the fulfillment of Isaiah's lavish prophetic vision (Isa. 55:1). At the end of each of the letters to the seven churches (Rev. 2–3), Jesus made a promise of reward to the one **who overcomes** (21:7). Here those rewards are encompassed in the comprehensive promise **will inherit all this** (Greek, *these things*). Infinitely more important is the promise of eternal family relationship: "I will be their God and they will be my children" (v. 7 NRSV). The reason some will be left out (v. 8) is not that God desires their exclusion, but that they will reject forever God's gracious offer of inclusion.

The Lamb Is the Lamp (Rev. 21:22–27)

Verses 9–21 comprise a vivid description of the external beauty of the New Jerusalem, the "bride" (vv. 2, 9). By verse 22, John, in his vision, had passed through one of the gates of pearl and entered into the city.

A striking feature of this paragraph is John's statements about what is *not* in the city. The Holy City has no temple, no need of sun or moon, no shutting of its gates, because it has no night, and nothing or no one impure within it. Each of these deserves further comment.

The traditional translation of verse 22 is both plausible and understandable. Yet given that John's native language was not Greek, but Hebrew or Aramaic, and given the presence in the last clause of a singular verb form, we also could translate, "I did not see a sanctuary in the city, for the Lord God Almighty, even the Lamb, is its sanctuary." John's statement in the next verse that **the Lamb is its lamp** (v. 23) would lend credibility to this translation, also. Whether John was speaking here of God the Father and God the Son or just of God the Son, his words emphasize the deity of the Lamb, and the oneness of the Godhead, in accordance with the language of verse 5.

WORDS FROM WESLEY

Revelation 21:22

The Lord God and the Lamb are the temple of it—He fills the new heaven and the new earth. He surrounds the city and sanctifies it, and all that are therein. He is all in all. (ENNT)

God's presence in the city, continuously and immediately among God's people, will make a sanctuary of physical materials unnecessary. This brings to mind Jesus' prophecy of His crucifixion. The temple of His body would be destroyed, but in three days He would raise it again (John 2:19–22).

The sun and moon, of course, are the light bearers by day and by night (Gen. 1:16). God's continuous presence in the city will make them unnecessary. **The glory of God** (Rev. 21:23) suggests the daytime, and **its lamp** (v. 23) suggests the night, except that the city does not experience night (v. 25). Moreover, many of John's readers and hearers, earlier in their lives, would have worshiped the sun and moon. This astonishing prediction of their retirement would have been another confirmation of their status as fellow creatures of the one and only true God. The absence of night will mean, also, that the **gates** of the city will not **be shut** (v. 25). Since city gates are shut at night to keep out danger, this means nothing ever again will threaten the safety and peace of God's people.

When they walk in righteousness, **nations** and **kings** (v. 24) exhibit God-created **splendor . . . glory and honor** (vv. 24, 26). When the city of God descends upon the earth, all will find their rightful and proper places within it. Thus will fulfill another of Isaiah's eschatological prophecies: "Nations will come to your light" (Isa. 60:3).

Nothing impure, whether things, ideas, events, or people, **will ever enter** (Rev. 21:27) this city. Henceforth, the city, God's people, and all the rest of God's creation will be restored to the purity of perfectly loving relationships God intended from the beginning. As noted above, no human being will be kept out by God's design or desire. All who will may have their **names . . . written in the Lamb's book of life** (v. 27), and dwell in the light of God's presence forever.

DISCUSSION

Discuss what you think heaven will be like.

1. Biblical scholars can't agree if heaven is "out there" or if it is right here, but not visible to our human eyes. What do you think?

2. No matter where heaven is, it is a state where "the dwelling of God is with men, and he will live with them" (Rev. 21:3). How does simply God's presence create a heavenly place?

3. What must be overcome if we are to inherit all this?

4. How has the message of heaven—and particularly the book of Revelation—given those living under persecution power to overcome?

5. John declared that God *is* light, and Revelation 21:23–24 note that God and the Lamb provide the light of heaven. What characteristics of light does God exhibit?

6. What is the significance that heaven's gate will never close?

7. What would life be like with "nothing impure . . . shameful or deceitful" (v. 27)?

8. How is this purity assured in heaven?

9. What is your idea of heaven after reading this study? Is it the same or different than what you previously thought?

PRAYER

Father, You supervised the creation of all things, and You will supervise the final consummation of all things. Remind us often of the hope we have in You and You alone. Prepare us now for our eternal life with You in heaven—in our worship, our service, and our focus on You alone.

COME, LORD JESUS

Revelation 22:1–6, 12–21

Christ will return soon.

This final chapter of Revelation—and the Bible—brings everything that preceded it to a focal point. Jesus will return and everything on earth will be impacted accordingly. Preparation through personal acceptance of Christ and His plan of salvation is the most important step one can take.

Throughout Revelation, John had been encouraging believers to prepare for the end times. He combined warnings with counsel to get us ready for all that is to come. An angel gave John a glimpse into the New Jerusalem in chapters 21 and 22 as a final encouragement for holy living and spiritual preparation. By sharing his experience with us, he helped us to determine the important from the insignificant. As you study this climactic chapter of Scripture, you will be motivated to focus your attention on the things that matter most.

COMMENTARY

Some observations from the previous study bear restating here. The context of Revelation 21–22 is the whole Bible, beginning with Genesis 1–2. This is the basis of the observation that God's creation-redemption relationship with the human race began in the garden of Eden and ends in the New Jerusalem. The Tree of Life was a focal point of the garden; now John saw it within the Holy City. Another reminder: The final enemies, death and Hades, have been dismissed forever (20:14). All is won; all is finished; all is new; all is joy; all is shalom, God's perfect peace.

Still, this was a vision of the future, given to an elderly exile at the end of the first century, in a time of intense pressure for the saints of God to bow to pretensions of divinity on the part of the emperor in Rome. Though the pretenders no longer bear the title "Caesar," the question still confronts us today: Will we worship the present world system, or will we live and die in the confidence that Jesus Christ alone is Lord and God?

Water of Life, Tree of Life, City of Light (Rev. 22:1–6)

Much of Revelation 21 is a general description of the Holy City, the New Jerusalem. These first verses of Revelation 22 complete this visionary description with John's report of seeing two of the city's most important features: **the river of the water of life** (v. 1) and **the tree of life** (v. 2). John's relatively short notice here draws on (but does not copy) a longer, more detailed description in Ezekiel 47:1–12.

Ezekiel had described the river as flowing "out from under the threshold of the temple" (Ezek. 47:1). In John's vision, the river flowed **from the throne of God and of the Lamb** (Rev. 22:1); God's real and immediate presence in the city means there is no further need of a temple. (Compare 21:22.)

The fact that the water of the river is **clear as crystal** (22:1) testifies to its purity. This water is good to drink. It will not destroy life; rather, it will give life.

John did not place a period either before or after the first phrase of verse 2. However, this punctuation may not be crucial. The only way for the **tree of life** to stand **on each side of the river** is for several, or many, individual specimens of this tree to line the banks of the river. Whether John intended to describe the river flowing, or the multiple specimens of the Tree of Life growing, **down the middle of the great street of the city** (v. 2), we should envision a great boulevard. The river is in the center; or hundreds of trees line its banks; the two great lanes of the boulevard flank the rows of trees on their outward sides, away from the river in the center.

All cities in John's day were tiny by modern standards. Not even Rome had broad streets with rows of trees down their centers. Moreover, in antiquity, when water ran down the center of a major street, it was the water of a combined storm-sewer channel covered away from view by stone paving. If John's vision seems heavenly but plausible to the modern mind, it seemed wildly impossible to his contemporaries — except by divine action which, of course, was John's intent.

The Tree of Life is mentioned first in Genesis 2:9. As noted in Genesis 3:22–24, God drove the first human pair from the garden of Eden so they no longer could eat of the Tree of Life and live forever in their newly fallen state. John's vision here, then, really means the human race is to be given access again to the Tree of Life, as another of the innumerable benefits of Christ's saving death. Now, however, it is to be not just one tree, but many trees; not just one fruit, but twelve fruits, one for each month — both abundance and variety are emphasized in this report of the tree's miraculous fruitfulness.

Immediately following as it does John's report of renewed access to the Tree of Life, the next promise, **No longer will there be any curse** (Rev. 22:3), should draw our attention back to Genesis 3. It is important to note that in no way — not even in their fall — did God pronounce any curse upon either the man or the woman, together the crown of God's earthly creation. John's promise of the removal of every curse, then, refers first to the renewed bounty of the earth. Of course, it includes also the reversal of the deadly *effects* upon the redeemed of all curses, whether imposed then or later.

WORDS FROM WESLEY
Revelation 22:3

"There shall be no more curse; but they shall see his face" (22:3, 4) — shall have the nearest access to, and thence the highest resemblance of, Him. This is the strongest expression in the language of Scripture, to denote the most perfect happiness. "And his name shall be on their foreheads"; they shall be openly acknowledged as God's own property, and His glorious nature shall most visibly shine forth in them. (WJW, vol. 5, 181)

In the early chapters of Revelation, the Lamb is not on the throne. Now, in the culmination of all things, the Lamb *is* seated with God upon the heavenly throne. Already here, John expressed the firm conviction that Jesus Christ, the slain, risen, and conquering Lamb (*not* Caesar in Rome) was, is, and ever shall be God.

In the kingdoms of John's day, privileged servants were those whose positions and duties allowed them to see the king's face, that is, to serve him in the palace and around the throne every day. In the heavenly city, all the redeemed **will see his face** (v. 4). Taking into account the whole of biblical revelation, God's human **servants** (v. 3) then will rejoice in the privilege of being part of God's family, even to the point of wearing in awe and reverence **his name** upon our **foreheads** (v. 4), secure in the love and grace that has engraved also Zion's name, representative of all the saints, upon His palm (Isa. 49:16).

The repetition (compare Rev. 21:23) of the promise that **the Lord God will give them light** (22:5) is a signal of its surety. In the Bible, as in much of literature, repetition denotes emphasis, an invitation to confidence in what is being asserted.

They will reign for ever and ever (v. 5). It is not necessary for non-musicians, for example, to worry that we will sit around all day in heaven, doing nothing but playing harps. God's nature is to create, to work, and to take joy in what God does, in what God creates. We cannot now say what all this will look like, but we can be confident that to reign with God eternally will be to learn to do at least some of what we have seen, and will see, God do. We will not become God or gods, but we will work—and rejoice in work—with God, as God's sons and daughters, as Jesus' younger brothers and sisters.

WORDS FROM WESLEY
Revelation 22:5

Surely there is no darkness in that city of God. Is it not expressly said (Rev. 22:5), "There shall be no night there?" Indeed they have no light from the sun; but "the Lord giveth them light," So it is all day in heaven, as it is all night in hell! On earth we have a mixture of both. Day and night succeed each other, till earth shall be turned to heaven. . . . They that are "before the throne of God serve him day and night," speaking after the manner of men, "in his temple" (Rev. 7:15); that is, without any interval. As wicked spirits are tormented day and night without any intermission of their misery; so holy spirits enjoy God day and night without any intermission of their happiness. (WJW, vol. 6, 210)

These words are trustworthy and true (v. 6) is another repetition, this one from 21:5; there the affirmation was spoken by the One "seated on the throne." That John heard it this time from the mouth of the angel is a reminder that angels, or messengers, speak the words of the One who sends them.

Verse 6 begins the epilogue to Revelation; the visions proper are ended. Their purpose was and is **to show his servants the things that must soon take place** (22:6). Knowing what the issues really are, God's servants then and now may take courage, and encourage each other, to stand firm in the faith when persecutions arise. Kept in and by the One who has overcome death and hell already, we too may overcome.

Alpha and Omega, Bright Morning Star (Rev. 22:12–17)

Here is the second of three times in this short epilogue where Jesus said, **"Behold, I am coming soon!"** (v. 12). The other places are near the beginning (v. 7) and near the end (v. 20); the third time, "Behold" is replaced with "Yes!" making for an even greater emphasis. This promise is as emphatic as a single passage can make it, and the fact that this is the last literary unit of the Bible lends the promise even greater weight.

"Without delay" instead of **soon** may encompass both the idea of a speedy return. Remembering that Jesus will return on God's eternal timetable, not on an earthly, temporal one—even the nearly two millennia since this promise was given—is **soon**. Another thousand years or more would be soon by God's eternal measure. And we may be sure that when God the Father gives the word, God the Son will come speedily!

I will give . . . according to what each **has done** (v. 12) is not a denial of salvation by God's grace alone. The faithful will receive rewards out of God's gracious bounty, as Scripture promises from beginning to end, knowing we will not deserve them. The faithless will realize the only possible end of their own desires and intentions, eternal separation from God—at their behest, not God's.

In Revelation 21:5, the One "seated on the throne" identified himself as the "Alpha and the Omega, the Beginning and the End" (v. 7). Here (22:13) Jesus was speaking, using this title of himself; as mentioned in the previous study, in other places (see 1:8) it may be used of God the Father or, possibly, it may refer there also to Jesus.

WORDS FROM WESLEY
Revelation 22:12

I, Jesus Christ, *come quickly*—To judge the world, *and my reward is with me*—The rewards which I assign both to the righteous and the wicked are given at My coming, *to give to every man according as his work*—His whole inward and outward behaviour, *shall be.* (ENNT)

The contrast outlined in 22:14–15 is between those who accept God's gracious offer of cleansing, inside and out, and those who do not. Those who accept are given **the right to the tree of life** and entrance **into the city** (v. 14). Those who remain outside could have accepted the same free gift; it is (or was) offered to them, as well. They remain outside by their choice, not God's. The four specific sets of sinful behaviors are examples; they reside, with others, in the all-inclusive descriptor, **everyone who loves and practices falsehood** (v. 15).

By nature and definition, God, God's words, and God's actions are "trustworthy and true" (21:5; 22:6). To place oneself outside the grace of God's reality is to embrace falsehood. In the end, falsehood can lead only to destruction, because it refuses the only reality, the only power by which life exists, the grace of God's sustaining power. (Compare Col. 1:17.) If one rejects the Author and Giver of life, what is left but death?

The Root and the Offspring of David (Rev. 22:16) is a reference to the prophecy of Isaiah 11:1, 10. **The bright Morning Star** (Rev. 22:16) goes all the way back to Balaam's oracle of Numbers 24:17. **The free gift of the water of life** (Rev. 22:17) refers to "the river of the water of life" (v. 1); it also marks the fulfillment of Isaiah's prophetic vision (Isa. 55:1), and reminds the reader that in His earthly ministry Jesus also had promised water to the thirsty (John 4:14; 6:35; 7:37–38).

Warning and Benediction (Rev. 22:18–21)

Warnings against tampering with a finished composition, whether in a book or a public inscription, were common over many centuries in western Asia and the eastern Mediterranean. These warnings against adding to or taking away from (vv. 18–19) are intended only for this book of Revelation, though in the Sermon on the Mount Jesus had expressed a similar caution with reference to the Pentateuch or even, perhaps, to the whole of the Old Testament (Matt. 5:17–20).

Revelation 22:20 records the third of the **I am coming soon** statements. Here, we see also a prayer of John, which well may be the prayer of every one of God's people, at some point in each life, and in many of history's crisis moments: **Amen. Come, Lord Jesus** (v. 20).

Revelation begins, in its first three chapters, with many of the marks of written epistles of the first century. This concluding benediction-farewell (v. 21) reminds us we still are reading a letter. That John prayed this personal benediction for every reader, modern as well as ancient, is a precious thought.

WORDS FROM WESLEY
Revelation 22:21

The grace—The free love of the Lord Jesus, and all its fruits, be with all who thus long for His appearing. (ENNT)

DISCUSSION

Reflect on your journey through the book of Revelation. Discuss what impacted you the most.

1. The new heaven and new earth will restore the perfection of the garden of Eden. What do you think that would that look like?

2. Throughout Scripture, water has been a powerful symbol. What are ways the Bible has used to describe water and rivers as symbols?

3. How does the image described into today's Scripture fulfill those images?

4. Fruit is also used throughout Scripture as word pictures. Can you name some examples?

5. How are those images fulfilled in the book of Revelation?

6. Why were Adam and Eve prevented from eating of the Tree of Life? What is the significance of the Tree of Life's appearance in this heavenly vision?

7. What were the consequences of the "curse" following the fall in Genesis 3? How are these reversed in Revelation 22?

8. What kinds of people are allowed into heaven? What kinds of people are excluded from heaven?

9. If we took this vision of heaven seriously, how might it affect the way we organize ourselves as a church here on earth?

PRAYER

Our Father who art in heaven, hallowed be thy name. Thy kingdom come!

WORDS FROM WESLEY WORKS CITED

ENNT: *Explanatory Notes upon the New Testament,* by John Wesley, M.A. Fourth American Edition. New York: J. Soule and T. Mason, for the Methodist Episcopal Church in the United States, 1818.

PW: *The Poetical Works of John and Charles Wesley.* Edited by D. D. G. Osborn. 13 vols. London: Wesleyan-Methodist Conference Office, 1868.

WJW: *The Works of John Wesley.* Third Edition, Complete and Unabridged. 14 vols. London: Wesleyan Methodist Book Room, 1872.

OTHER BOOKS IN THE
WESLEY BIBLE STUDIES SERIES

Genesis (available February 2015)
Exodus (available April 2015)
Leviticus through Deuteronomy (available June 2015)
Joshua through Ruth (available June 2015)
1 Samuel through 2 Chronicles (available February 2015)
Ezra through Esther (available April 2015)
Job through Song of Songs (available February 2015)
Isaiah (available April 2015)
Jeremiah through Daniel (available February 2015)
Hosea through Malachi (available June 2015)
Matthew
Mark
Luke (available September 2014)
John
Acts (available September 2014)
Romans
1–2 Corinthians (available September 2014)
Galatians through Colossians and Philemon
1–2 Thessalonians (available September 2014)
1 Timothy through Titus
Hebrews
James
1–2 Peter and Jude
1–3 John
Revelation

Now Available in the
Wesley Bible Studies Series

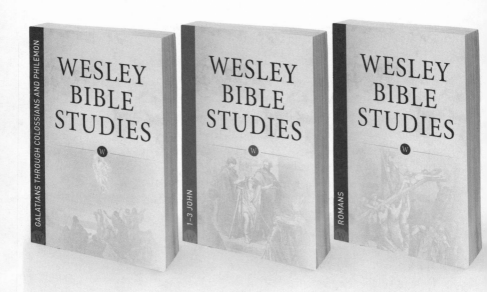

Each book in the Wesley Bible Studies series provides a thoughtful and powerful survey of key Scriptures in one or more biblical books. They combine accessible commentary from contemporary teachers, with relevantly highlighted direct quotes from the complete writings and life experiences of John Wesley, along with the poetry and hymns of his brother Charles. For each study, creative and engaging questions foster deeper fellowship and growth.

Galatians through Colossians and Philemon
978-0-89827-864-4
978-0-89827-865-1 (e-book)

Romans
978-0-89827-854-5
978-0-89827-855-2 (e-book)

1–3 John
978-0-89827-856-9
978-0-89827-857-6 (e-book)

wphonline.com
1.800.493.7539

SPEND SOME LOVE

SPEND SOME LOVE

AND OTHER TIPS

ON

INCARNATION

Margaret Dulaney

LISTEN WELL PUBLISHING

Paintings by Robin Phillips

Edited by Aina Barten
Copy edited by Hayden Saunier
Book design by Brooke Koven

ISBN 978-0-9986023-7

First Printing, 2022

Dedicated to the Great, Big,
(oddly lovable) Family of Man.

CONTENTS

PREFACE   *3*

1. *The Animating Properties of Love*   *7*

2. *Prayer*   *13*

3. *The Laundry*   *19*

4. *The Real Secret*   *26*

5. *The Houses of Our Souls*   *32*

6. *Measuring God*   *39*

7. *Not Mine*   *45*

8. *All God's Children*   *51*

9. *Wishes*   *58*

10. *Paper Snowflakes*   *64*

11. *Pilgrimage*   *70*

12. *A Measure of Meaning*   *76*

13. *To Keep the Sabbath*   *82*

14. *Small Miracles*   *88*

15. *Lifting the Veil*   94

16. *Pyramid Scheme*   101

17. *Just Right*   107

18. *From Here*   113

19. *Hesitation*   119

20. *Pinball Mind*   125

21. *Step, Stop, Turn Back, Lift*   131

22. *Our Big Beautiful Selves*   137

23. *The Pasture*   144

24. *The Key to Confidence*   150

25. *Good Cheer*   156

26. *When to Take Your Temperature*   162

27. *Stage Serenity*   168

28. *The Eleventh Hour*   173

29. *Spend Some Love*   180

30. *The Gifts of Aging*   186

31. *Light Work*   193

32. *Slow Prayers*   199

33. *Labor of Love*   205

SPEND SOME LOVE

PREFACE

SINCE I began to explore my musings on the divine, I have nursed the fantasy of being able to write for atheists. The problem is, I use the G-word too much. The reason I have never plunged deeply into any organized religion is that I have a fierce repulsion of becoming exclusionary. Of course, I know that this division of insiders and outsiders is not a given among traditional believers. There are many who could never accept that those outside of their churches, synagogues, mosques are any less loved and cared for by the G-word than their fellow insiders, but even a hint of the club-atmosphere will have me heading for the woods where I tend most often to have long conversations with the G-word.

My suspicion is that if we could all substitute the G-word for the L-word (LOVE) we would find common ground. Think of it: Love, like God, is impossible to prove, yet we have all felt love. Even if we loved for only a moment, even if we felt it only once and for a puppy, we know love.

If one follows the promptings of Love to perform a selfless act of kindness, does it matter the language used to describe the impulse? If a scientist spends his life attempting to come up with a cure for an illness that has caused suffering to his fellow brothers and sisters, does it matter his theological leanings? Does it matter if he is consciously acting for what you or I might consider a divinely inspired impulse? I don't believe so, and I suspect that the great Spirit of Love is pleased with any act of love.

This book is a collection of essays on Love, with a capital L. It is an offering of a few drops into an ocean of ideas of ways in which one might spend this inexhaustible gift.

I

The Animating Properties
of Love

WHEN THE Austrian philosopher and mystic Rudolf Steiner, who lectured on just about every subject imaginable around the turn of the twentieth century, was asked what the next great breakthrough in medicine might be, he answered that the medical community would discover that "The heart is not a pump. The blood drives the heart, not the heart the blood."

I like to picture a waterwheel.

If this is true, and it resonates with my thinking, then what is it that causes our blood to flow? What is behind this mystery we call life?

If you have seen a human corpse, you will have witnessed the utter absence of the life force. I can understand the wisdom behind the open casket, for it demonstrates, without any doubt, that the spirit is not there. A body without its animating blood flow is like a pile of clothes left in a heap. It is perhaps the emptiest thing I have ever beheld.

Many years ago, I was visiting my brother in Kentucky when the subject of God arose, as it often does when we are together. I told him that I didn't believe I could raise my arm without God. To demonstrate, I raised my arm in the air, and then let it flop back down to my side.

That afternoon I took a brief nap. Falling easily into a deep sleep, I was awakened by my arm being gently raised by some unknown force and let go to fall back on the bed.

"What the heck?" I thought, as I shot up to stare at my arm. That evening I told my brother about the strange occurrence and he reminded me of what I had said earlier about God and my utter dependence on this animating being for my existence.

But what is this spirit that enlivens us? Who, and what is God?

George MacDonald, the nineteenth-century Scottish writer, who Evelyn Underhill considered "the grandfather of all Christian writers," has written, "What is the deepest in God? His power? No, for power could not make him what we mean when we say God... A being whose essence was only power would be such a negation of the divine that no righteous worship could be offered him, his service must be fear, and fear only." I think of a Stalin, a Hitler. No, MacDonald continues, "In a word, God is love. Love is the deepest depth, the essence of his nature, at the root of all his being."

When I think of what stimulates me, what wakes me in the morning, pops me happily out of bed—my husband will attest to my being annoyingly cheerful in the morning—I realize it has everything to do with love. One of the first things to love is the sun trying to break through the darkness and into the bedroom window, this, along with our cat Button who is awakened by the whoosh that I presume my spirit makes when it returns to the body. Not two seconds after I gain consciousness, often before my eyes have opened, I will hear Button's feet hit the floor, even if she has been sleeping in the bedroom above ours. I lie still and listen as she makes her way from where she had been sleeping to our bed to leap up on me for her morning greeting. After some time spent in this love fest, I will get up and brush my teeth, and head downstairs to greet my dogs. It seems they too have heard the whoosh of my spirit's return from wherever it has been while my body lay in deep sleep, as they too have popped awake and made their way to the foot of the stairs. I see their looks of wild expectation in the half-light and head down the stairs to witness their fits of ecstasy over my making it through the night, the joy of which throws them into a full-body wag, as if someone had hold of their tails and pumped these handles back and forth. When I reach them, they mash their foreheads against my knees. "Thank God," they seem to say, "Thank God, you are still with us."

In speaking to a friend about someone dear to me who is going through a devastating depression and can barely leave his bed, she asked, "Does he have a job to go to? Some reason to get out of bed?" "No," I answered, but added, "But it seems to me that even those who do have jobs, and who suffer from depression, are not necessarily moved to exit their beds because they are employed." Our country has witnessed several public examples of those with seemingly highly engaging careers who have chosen to end their lives.

It follows that a job has no more power to lift us from the bed than a popsicle. A job that one loves is a different story. A job that is supporting the family that you love, a job that allows you to feed your loving animals, that allows you to maintain your beloved home—these may be reasons to leap from the horizontal, but not just a job.

So, what is it that causes the rivers of blood-life to course through our veins?

The eighteenth-century mystic Emanuel Swedenborg wrote that love was not only the power that drove the life of man during his time on Earth, but that love was the force that would drive the soul through all of eternity. He wrote that our "affections" (a word he uses for small earthly loves), were fed by God's love, that even the smallest affection, held for the briefest moment, an encounter of kindness between two people in a checkout line, for instance, is infused by the love of God. He believed that our expressions of love were essentially God loving through us: that the love that a mother feels for her child is from the same great source that motivates a human toward the smallest act of kindness. And more to the point, Swedenborg tells us that if there were no overreaching, underpinning love of God, there would be no existence. It is love that animates all of life.

"Love in its essence is spiritual fire," he wrote. He believed that God was like the sun, whose fire and heat were love. Life on earth could not exist without the sun, nor could we exist without the love of God.

The many clichés that speak to this truth, "Love makes the world go 'round" "Love is all there is," "God is love," and so on, tend to weaken its power to affect us, but I suspect our hearts understand the concept profoundly.

We could not live if we were not loved. We could not exist if God were not loving us into existence. It is love that brings us into life and sustains us and it is love that will eventually take us home to more life.

2

Prayer

I HAVE, FOR some time, wanted to begin a prayer circle, but remain stymied over the organizational details. I wrote a piece several years ago, which resides now in the Listen Well archives, called *The Anonymous Ones*. The essay explores the notion that there might be groups of concerned souls around the world that regularly meet for prayer in what I will refer to here as the prayer ether, a sacred place of connection, where they bring their hopes and wishes for the health of the planet and for the spiritual health of all the souls that occupy the Earth.

I recently read a man's account of being given a piece of advice during a heavenly vision: if just twenty people gathered to pray for peace for their nation, that nation might be saved from war. However unfathomable this idea might seem, I do believe in the great power in prayer.

This morning on my walk in the woods, I began to think of how I could initiate a prayer circle. I considered the time that I regularly pray, from approximately 7:30 to 8:30 Eastern Standard Time in the U.S. I wondered whether I could ask those who wished to join me to pray at the same time. But I don't believe that the efficacy of prayer is dictated by time. We incarnated ones are inside of time, but our loved ones on the other side are not, nor is the one to whom we pray. Why should a prayer be restricted by the constraints of time?

I considered a place where we might meet, or perhaps where we might imagine we are gathering. I wondered whether there was a holy spot on the earth where we might come together in our imaginations to send up our prayers. But prayer is not limited by any particular place. A prayer delivered from a jail cell is as powerful as one delivered from a synagogue.

I thought of asking like-minded souls to join my group, but why should I add exclusivity to the directives for my prayer group? All souls in prayer are heard.

I thought of coming up with a weekly subject over

which my group might pray, but all prayers are important, from those to find your lost cat to those for peace between nations.

I began to see my gathering of concerned individuals as more of an invitation to step into the current of prayer that already exists, this river of concern for all living things that is sent out from the hearts of men and women around the earth.

This current, I imagined, is much like the movement of water around the planet: continuous, unending, always moving, moving. I began to think of all of the movement around the earth, of the waters, the wind, the movement of the clouds, forming, collecting, and finally releasing their water, to be gathered, and released, around and around the world, constantly in motion. Like the waters from the high mountains, careening down falls, shooting through gullies, gorging, shaping the land, racing through streams into rivers, then widening and running to the sea, only to be taken up into the clouds to complete the cycle again and again. Circling, circling like the movement of prayers and the answers to prayers.

This constant motion is reflected in the movement of planets and stars and galaxies, and in our own bodies with our blood flowing through our veins, feeding our bodies, bringing healing to our wounds, restoring our bodies, our minds.

And, I realized, all of this movement, this life-giving motion, is powered by spirit. If God departed from our universe, all of the movement of life would go still, black, blank.

When my husband wakes in the middle of the night and can't go back to sleep, and if I manage to wake up fully enough to notice, I will rest my hand on his head, hoping this will comfort him so that he will fall back asleep. Several years ago, I thought I should add prayer to this ritual, and prayed for him to fall asleep, while my hand rested on his head.

One night, I thought I would call on the angelic kingdom to help out. I asked that a special angel come and lay his or her hand on mine. "Please come and rest your hand on mine and help to put Matt back to sleep," I asked.

I don't believe it happened the first time I asked, but after trying the experiment several times, I felt something on my hand, a sensation of sorts, as if another hand were on top of mine. It was subtle but undeniable. This feeling of pressure on my hand has been a recurring phenomenon for seven years or so. Sometimes the feeling is quite pronounced. And, though it often results in Matt falling asleep, this result is not guaranteed.

One night recently, I lay my hand on Matt's head, asking for help, when I felt the familiar feeling. I thanked whomever it was that had come to our aid, and lay, enjoying the sensation for a few moments, when a thought arose in my head. To be clear, it was more as if the thought was tossed into my mind, harvested from where I cannot tell, for I had not been anywhere near its subject for years. It was a negative thought about someone I had not thought of for quite some time, carrying with it a grievance that I assumed I had put far behind me. Seduced by the old thing, I followed it into criticism, "Yeah," I thought, "that really was an outrage, blah, blah, blah..." when pop! the feeling on my hand abruptly ceased.

It was as if I had been hung up on. Slam!

"Ah, I get it," I responded in thought, "so faultfinding closes the door."

I went on to apologize to whomever it was who had joined me from the heavens, but to no avail, I could not reconnect. My hand remained the only one on my husband's head that night.

Such a valuable lesson! Thoughts colored by criticism serve as a dam to the waters of prayer and aid.

In thinking more about this moment, I must assume that the power behind the prayers that rise from this world is love.

I suspect love might be the only ingredient necessary to lift a prayer. Love of one's country, for instance, would allow the hope for peace between one's nation and another to find an answer. Love of another person would allow our prayers to be heard and allow for the flow of aid and comfort.

If, when asking for help for my sleepless husband, I focus on my love of him, I imagine the aid will come, but if I add any critical thinking such as the fact that he stayed up too late watching a violent movie, and how of course that would disturb anyone's sleep, the heavens will not bother listening to me. Why should they?

This brings me back to my prayer circle, which I am hoping to start this moment. But first, let us toss out the rules. We may pray at any time, we may pray in any place, and all minds are like-minded. We may pray for the tiniest insect, or for the peace of the world. We may call our prayers anything we want: a wish, a hope, a dream, a miracle. We may break every presumed rule but one: Love.

Love must be present. Love surrounding every concern. Love lifting.

3 *The Laundry*

MY HUSBAND and I went to a party recently for a friend who was turning eighty. We have known the family for some time, have heard much about its history, its function and dysfunction. I had been close to this man's wife, who had died two years earlier, and the celebration seemed part party and part wake. The kids, all in their middle age, gave toasts and performed skits. One fine routine involved two of the daughters lip-synching to the Lonely Goatherd song from the Sound of Music. "High on a hill was a lonely goatherd, yo-la-ey-oh-do-la-ey-oh-do-lay-e-oh." It was conceived in their middle-school years and requested by their father. Nothing could have been a better testament to a happy childhood. Several of the grandchildren performed as well. It was a grand gathering with the evening eventually degrading into a wild squirt-gun battle between the generations.

On the way home from the party Matt and I talked about family. No matter the challenges, the rights and wrongs, the disagreements, commonality, separation, frustration, no matter what is experienced among the handful of souls that make up our families, I suspect it's only the love that survives. It's only love that is ultimately rounded up and measured, if measured is the word, more like celebrated. Everything else, I have to assume, will come out in the laundry.

We know a couple that had a two-year-old daughter when they discovered that they were going to have another child. When they went to check the health of the new baby, the doctor discovered three heartbeats. They had triplet boys. Theirs was a solid marriage, but there had to have been moments of great stress, raising these children. They lived far from their parents and had very busy schedules. When the boys were about nine their mother grew ill with cancer and by the time they were fourteen, she had died. Several years later my husband was talking to the father, when he said, "I'm good. We're good, my wife and me. We're good with each other now." It wasn't that they weren't good with each other before, but he felt that they had continued to understand one another after her death.

I have to believe that love, all love continues to grow in purity into eternity. You hear people say, "Oh, I wish I had told my father how much I loved him before he died." My answer: "Tell him now. Go and find a field, a forest, a quiet room, and tell him that you love him. Don't waste another moment in regret."

I can't imagine death stands a chance against the progress of love. Like a tsunami to a cobweb, love obliterates everything in its path.

My brother's wife died very suddenly over a year ago. Since her passing, he is occasionally haunted by what sounds to me like his inability during their life together to offer her 300 percent of his support, rather than the 289 percent that he was able to muster. The good news is, he talks to her. Once, in a car—cars, by the way, are excellent places to speak with those who have passed through the Great Door—once, while my brother was having a conversation with his wife, he suddenly thought to ask, "Do you even hear me when I talk to you?" At which point a bookmark that had belonged to his wife and which was housed firmly in a book in the back seat of his car, worked its way out of the book, rose up and floated between the two seats to land gently on his knee.

Mourning a human being can be full of challenges, complicated by a checkered history of mood swings and mistakes, with things we wish we hadn't said, things we wish we had said, actions we regret. But these can always be healed. There is an eternity of time to heal our relationships. Love isn't frozen by death, in fact, some argue that it is set free.

The great Scottish writer George MacDonald had this to say about death and its effect on love...

"I believe that the death of those we love is in order to bring our hearts nearer. I am confident, that in millions of cases, the love that would never be perfected without death, is perfected by death, and that death is just the ripening autumn sun. It ripens the love that could not get to its perfection and simplicity here, the bodily presence carrying it only so far."

But how to begin to accomplish this?

Perhaps the first step toward bringing this love to harvest is to look at our history with the loved one and to focus on those moments where the love was purest, where we felt unconditional care from a parent, keen sacrifice from a spouse, real tenderness from a friend, surprising support from a sibling. Take these moments and leave the rest.

Too often our attention is on the dysfunction, the difficult moments of our history, so that we lose sight of the astonishing love-filled ones.

Try and cut away the voices and opinions of those who share your history. Try and hush the judgments of siblings, parents, friends, partners, therapists and look at these moments through the eyes of love only. Look where love incarnated, where love first showed its shy spirit. Look where joy cracked through the surface of your life in the presence of this person, where humor lifted you, beauty overtook you. Look for the times when you ran to the heart of this person, knowing that you would find safe haven.

I am thinking of a time when I was 19 and home for the holidays and I caught a stomach flu that lasted almost a week. On day three, my mother brought me a bowl of oatmeal. It wasn't that she hadn't been checking on me, hadn't shown her concern, hadn't made sure I was hydrated, but my mother had never learned to cook anything more than toast during her life. There she stood, steaming bowl in hand, offering me something that had required boiling and stirring. I was overwhelmed with the love behind that gesture.

As you can see, the gesture doesn't have to be filled with grandeur, just love.

Search for those times when the crust of prejudice, shallow principles, small opinions, superiority, everything that might have served to condemn and separate fell away, and you will see that all that is left is one tender heart sharing another in equal tenderness.

Now imagine this: after the soul has gone through the transition of this world into the next, nothing but this tenderness remains. Nothing of the history between this loved one and you that was not born of love is left. Nothing. It all came out in the laundry of death. Washed clean.

And, this soul, no longer father, mother, lover, child, brother, sister, this soul is all friend, just loving friend.

Now speak with that soul. Stand next to them, watch the sunset together, the moonrise, share something beautiful. Tell them the things that you are able to love because they loved them. Tell them the things you learned to hold dear because they held them dear. If you wish to apologize for any difficult history, you may do so, but the hope is that you will eventually arrive somewhere beyond the need for forgiveness. A place of gratitude and gladness.

"I wish you well," you will say to them.

"And I you," you will sense in response.

How simple it is to love someone through the eyes of love only.

4

The Real Secret

I HEARD A man interviewed on the radio who claimed to have made a remarkable discovery. He described himself as an ordinary man, holding down an ordinary desk job with little opportunity for creativity. He added that he had been unsuccessful in love for much of his life. He had dated, perhaps even married and divorced (I don't remember), but had never found what he considered to be true love. At some point in his middle years, he searched his history to learn why he had found so little joy in his life.

For much of his life, he reflected that at school, at work and in bed, he had been on a quest to be loved. And even though he had found those who were willing to love him, he was still unhappy, empty, and unfulfilled.

Clearly, being loved was not bringing him happiness. So, what was the answer...? Loving, he concluded. He realized that he was happy only while loving. Being loved without loving back held no joy whatsoever. Loving was the key.

I have read hundreds of near-death experiences and the consistent takeaway from those who have experienced these brushes with death is the promise that behind us, above us, beneath us, and beside us is a grand spirit of unconditional love. With this comes the understanding that no matter who you have become, no matter the dark deeds you have committed (excessive criticism, cruelty, even murder), no matter how you might feel about yourself, you are loved without condition.

Any judgment one feels in the presence of such love is from oneself, and not from this source of bottomless love. It seems we are loved beyond all comprehension.

Then what are we meant to do here? Why were we given life? If the object is not to win love, then what is it?

When I was young and first entered the theater as an actor, I believed that being hired in my chosen field would complete me. At some point I began to write plays and my focus switched from acting to having my plays produced. I believed that this would somehow fit all of the little pieces of myself together to make a legitimate whole and, of course, bring me happiness. I looked for recognition and, if I am going to be perfectly honest, I would have liked to be adored. Like Bob Hope, who in his nineties had a driver take him to an airport every morning to be recognized and loved, I was chasing something that would not have made me happy. I would have wakened one day and found myself in a place of emptiness.

I had a dream one night, actually a series of dreams, in which I walked the streets of a small town in Italy.

In about the fifth dream of this town, I began to recognize that I had been there before. "Oh, I'm in that Italian town again," I would think, "and I know where everything is. It's all so familiar. The Cathedral is down that street on the small piazza. The library is up that road on the hill." I know each little pasticceria and trattoria.

In the seventh dream of this town, I find myself again in the streets of this oddly familiar place. It is morning, and I stroll along the sidewalk without haste, taking in the scene around me, and begin to understand that I am not myself, not Margaret, but someone else. I am an Italian woman in her mid-forties, unmarried, and a schoolteacher. I was born in this place and have an apartment near the cathedral. I have been teaching the children of this town for the past twenty years or so. This is my home.

As I walk through the familiar streets, I take in the cars jammed along the sides of the narrow, stone sidewalks, cars that are current to the year in my waking life.

I move along, thinking the thoughts of this woman. I am this woman, or I and this woman are one. And, after a while, I have a sort of epiphany. It begins with a realization of how much I love the town that I have lived in all of my life. I love it as one would a beloved friend. The love increases and penetrates the buildings of the town to embrace all of the children whom I have taught over the years. I love them dearly. The love then multiplies and spills over to sustain every single soul who inhabits the town and, eventually, this vast love is everywhere around me, even tenderly holding the stones with which the town was built. I love the stones. I love the hills where these stones were unearthed. I am filled with love.

I think to myself, "My God, all of these years I hoped and longed for a man to come into my life and love me. I believed that this was the one thing that I lacked and mistakenly concluded that I had a half-empty life. How could I have believed this when this glorious possibility of love was all around me? How could I have believed this when there was so much for me to love?"

I basked in this electrifying state for several minutes before I woke up.

This was to be the final dream of the little Italian town. I have never had another.

My suspicion is that I was allowed, for some reason, to share in this Italian woman's mystical experience. The timing for me (in the middle of the night on the east coast of America) would coincide perfectly with the morning hours in Italy. The cars were current models. In other words, this was no past life experience. The dreams leading up to this morning seem in retrospect to build naturally to this revelation and were a preparation of sorts.

I have never had an epiphany of this intensity in my waking life. And, although I would cherish such an experience, perhaps this was enough, this sharing.

It remains a treasure.

5

The Houses of Our Souls

I've been reading a book written by a man who clinically died in his twenties and visited the other side. This man claims to have walked and talked with Jesus. And as sometimes occurs during these experiences, the two of them reviewed this man's life up to the moment of his near-death visit. I love such books and often write about the effects they have had on my thinking. For those who are as fond of such accounts as I am, the title is *Life After Heaven* by Steven Musick.

I hope I don't ruin the book for you by choosing to explore one of the many thoughts that the author brings up. I am particularly drawn to the distinction between our perspective on our personal histories and God's understanding of the same.

Mr. Musick raises the idea, which many of those who have had such experiences mention, that our thoughts and lives are more closely watched than we could ever imagine, and that our feelings are more deeply felt than even we have felt them. Along with this hair's breadth, ultra-sensitive connection to our histories, there is absolute understanding and compassion for us and our deficiencies and malfunctions. There is a reason for our behavior. There is always a reason. And we are forgiven. We were forgiven even before we acted. There can be sorrow around our transgressions and sympathy for our sufferings but there are no surprises. Our history, every inch of it, has been shared with the heavens and therefore our actions are not unexpected.

I presume that if we all were given an intimate view of each other's lives, if we understood one another completely, there could be no bewilderment over another's behavior. The only emotions left would be joy or sadness; sadness for the history that led to the behavior and joy at the overcoming of that history.

Steven Musick writes in his book that, though he remembered many of the difficult moments of his past and could see the effects that these encounters had on his behavior, and the subsequent effects that his behavior had on others, there were many more occurrences (slights, we might call them) of which he was not aware. He had not noticed them, or if he had, he did not see them as having the power to wound, to change his thinking and therefore alter the course of his life. The subtleties of this review were highly informative. Even the slightest criticism has power to alter our direction.

When I was eight years old my uncle died in a car accident. He was my mother's only sibling and was thirty when he left the world. I don't remember being terribly close to my uncle, though I did have a fondness for him. I didn't know the circumstances of his accident, just that he was alone, it was the middle of the night, and he drove his car into a tree. It was believed that he was killed instantly.

Ten years later, when I was eighteen and away at college, I had a dream about my uncle. He took me on a tour of the house in which he had grown up. Ushering me through the home with great deliberation, he allowed me time to study the details of each room: his parent's room, his room, his sister's (my mother's) room. At the end of this careful tour, he turned to me and said, "You see, this is why I drank. And, why I felt I could not remain in the world." I felt a profound sadness for his story and understood completely how difficult it was for him to remain on earth. When I woke, I had no memory of the history, just the message my uncle had wished to convey.

Before this dream, I had not heard that my uncle had developed a problem with alcohol, nor that he was particularly unhappy.

I waited until I traveled home for the holidays that year to ask my older siblings about our uncle and what the circumstance of his death had been. "Oh yes, he was a big partier, out almost every night," they assured me, "and the night he died, he had been at a party with Mom, where she had begged him to call it a night and go home, but he didn't heed her warning, and went to a local bar. Late that night he drove his car into a tree."

My grandmother once told me that when one dreams about walking around in someone's house, the house represents that person's soul. I was given the opportunity during my dream about my uncle to walk around in another's soul, something we are not able to do on Earth.

I have often wondered why my uncle chose to visit me that night. What might we have meant to one another if he had lived? I wonder if the riches of that relationship, having been removed from my history, were what inspired him to visit and explain, an apology of sorts. I look forward to getting to know him when I cross over into the next world.

If we could see our own histories with all of the whys revealed, all the roots of function and dysfunction, from grand to slight, I suspect we would have a perfect picture of our present attitude toward life. But there is more, and this is one of the great beauties of life on earth. It seems that all those wounds, all the little hurts and slights, can be used for good. This is so difficult to believe when you are only thirty, but this is the very material with which God works.

When I was in primary school the message that I took from most of my teachers was that I was unlikely ever to excel in reading and writing. I accepted this for many years until I left school altogether and began to choose my own reading material and, perhaps more important, began to read at my own pace (turtle-slow). I crawled my way through the brambles of my early challenges to a belief that I could acquire the necessary skills to express myself in the written word. Had I not been so challenged, I wonder whether I would have taken up the pen. Sometimes we need something to push against in order to move forward.

Mr. Musick uses the word "formative." Our souls are in a constant state of being formed. This is never-ending work.

If there were no God, if this life were just a patchwork of random hurts and periodic praise, our histories would hold no hope for us, would lead us nowhere, would have little power to enlighten. But there is a God, one who is always busy inside our lives spinning our difficulties into gold. The most dreadful circumstances can lead to the noblest conclusions: the enslaved person who gains his freedom can become an advocate for the enslaved, the abused can become a champion for the abused. Each of us can transcend our pasts, break the bounds of our histories, and discover a way to make our lives fruitful.

If we could only believe in the power of the heavens to aid us in our individual struggles, we might be liberated, and able to offer encouragement to others.

Considering how difficult it is to step far enough out of our own soul houses to see the subtleties of our histories, how little can we know of another soul? Our limited perspective should compel us to practice complete compassion for our brother's and sister's transgressions, no matter what their behavior. There must be a reason, a history of bruising or perhaps mental illness, that we cannot see.

And, of greater importance, there is the one working inside of our histories, our lives, one who is always spinning and spinning, spinning us into gold.

6

Measuring God

I READ A story recently about a man whose wife wished to divorce him. He did not want to part with her nor his children and so refused to leave the home, though she begged him to do so for months and months. I picture him lurking ghostlike in the basement, haunting the family with his gloomy presence.

The man was a member of a men's group and one of the members found an obscure piece of scripture in the Old Testament that read, "God hates divorce." This encouraged the men to believe that they knew precisely what God thought of their friend's situation, and they went to work directly in petitioning the heavens without a hint of doubt as to what might be best for the couple.

In discussing this story with a friend, the two of

us tried to imagine how the line "God hates divorce," might have crept its way into the Good Book.

"Hey," one of the scribes might have reacted while reading back over the week's work, "what the heck is this?"

Another scribe joins him and peers over his shoulder "God hates... Hey, wait a minute, whose handwriting is this?"

A third scribe walks over and studies the copy. He says, "Mordecai?"

All three turn to a corner of the room, and there sits the rejected Mordecai, disgruntled, guilty.

How can the Great Spirit of Love hate?

This reminds me of a story my brother tells from when he was in his twenties, and a friend said that she believed that God was often impatient with us when we did not progress as swiftly in our spiritual development as He would have liked. The idea haunted him. He spoke with a woman whom he much admired and asked her if she believed that God was ever impatient with us. Her answer was quite simple: "God has no faults."

I think this calls for a "duh."

I wonder whether most of our struggles on Earth have more to do with our ideas of God and how God works in the world than with anything else. Much of my own spiritual effort goes into trying to keep my view of God from shrinking. On many days I feel as if I am struggling with a giant rubber band around my soul that wants always to snap back into a tight, constricting chokehold.

When I was young, my ideas around this subject were quite small. When I experienced something that felt punishing—heartbreak, failure, humiliation—I would turn to God and ask what I might have done to deserve such a thing. As if to say, "I've been good! Why are you treating me this way?!" I would apply the same reasoning to stories I heard of a friend suffering or cataclysmic occurrences around the world. "Why did you send that illness to him, he's such a good person?" or, "Why did you not stop that argument before it turned into a World War?" As if God were some demented, unpredictable judge, handing down wildly unfair sentences: "That'll be five hundred years in purgatory for you! And you! Six years without cheese! And that one! Off with his limbs!"

I pray my view has expanded. I believe the rubber band is growing a bit flabbier, less likely to snap back and hit me in the eye.

Politics' involvement with religion has worked colossal damage to our understanding of the relative size of God. To suppose that this Grand Spirit is on one side or the other of our political debates is classic puny thinking. We imagine a restless, impatient, fretting god, having internal arguments over the latest struggles between conservatives and progressives. Nonsense. God wants us, not our petty opinions.

The audacity of my own cramped thinking will sometimes have me believing that I know exactly which side God is on. Like Anne in *Anne of Green Gables*, I will say of a neighbor, "I don't think we have the same God."

It takes diligence to push against the power of our narrowing views.

I picked up a book about forgiveness the other day and read the line "You have to DESERVE God's forgiveness."—not ask for it, mind you, deserve it. I had to keep from hurling the book across the room. This sort of thinking is crazy-making.

In the book *Into the Light*, written by the hospice doctor John Lerma, I read that the thing that most often hampers those near the end of their lives from making easy transitions to the next world is their feeling of guilt, their inability to forgive themselves. But how are they to forgive themselves if their idea of God is a stingy-hearted, relentlessly punitive schoolmarm with a list of rules as long as the Mississippi?

A friend once innocently remarked, "Well, of course, God will forgive many things, but not murder, right?"

Aaargh! This is God we're talking about! How could the Limitless One's capacity for forgiveness be limited?

I say this, but then my own rubber band will tighten around a story of injustice and I will imagine a heavenly tribunal sentencing some cold-hearted old judge to a thousand years in the next world's prison system. Or I will say of a politician who refuses to address the issue of gun control, "Woah, he's going to have a lot of blood on his hands when he reaches the end of his life." I picture this man, like Lady Macbeth, spending the rest of eternity wringing his stained hands.

Sometimes I get on a roll, handing down fantasy sentences for all sorts of transgressions, "Oh, that story almost makes me want to believe in hell, just so I can throw that guy in there." But, thankfully, eventually, I catch myself.

"No, stop!" I protest, "I do not follow this system. It is a big fat lie!"

"God is love! This I believe! God is forgiveness! God is all understanding!"

I feel the rubber band slacken and my heart rate slow.

I think of Rwanda, the genocide, the process of restitution, the forgiveness. A country filled with forgiveness. How did they manage this?

Without God, impossible. With God, inevitable.

7

Not Mine

S EVERAL YEARS ago, I hired a woman to help me with a project, and it went so swimmingly well that I recommended her to others. To abbreviate the story, some of my friends did not share my keen response to working with her and I received some rather irritated phone calls on the subject. I did feel a bit guilty but finally concluded that, after all, this woman wasn't mine. By that I mean she was her own person, and not mine to defend, apologize for, counter with praise. The fact is that each of us will behave differently with each new encounter, and although there are some temperaments that generally don't mix well with anyone, when paired with certain other humors they will act in striking harmony.

I try to be aware of not owning another in my dealings with everyone these days, both in action and thought. If I am concerned about someone, especially if I feel I know what that person should do to help himself or herself, I will repeat, "He is not mine. She is not mine."

No one belongs to another. Even children are only on loan, to be carried for a time and set back on their feet. I have a friend who tells me that she realizes that at some point she must be willing to "divorce" her children in order to help them to be independent. This is an almost herculean act of bravery on the part of a parent, to stand by while a child falls and fails, but it must eventually be performed, or the child will never find his footing, never find her balance. If the parent won't do this, the child must rip himself away, and that is usually less desirable. If neither will cut the cord, fate will step in and cause the tear. No one wants this, it's usually very ouchy.

It's always easier to see a lesson when it is headed in a friend's direction than when it's headed your own way. It's equally clear which lessons continue to return and return because the person has not learned from them.

Some friends will try and point out the obvious, try and describe what they are seeing, and others will leave the friend to figure it out on their own. I imagine there is a point of perfect balance between brutal honesty and detached apathy, I have never managed to stay there for very long, but I know it when I find it in others and gravitate toward those who can be both honest with me and healthily detached.

I do believe that, whether or not we are able to listen to our friends, ultimately it is God who changes us. "God is working his purpose out," as the old hymn goes, and all lessons are divinely gifted. If we are lucky, we have those around us who are willing to describe to us what we are unwilling to see ourselves, but in the end, it is God who hands us the lessons and helps us to learn them.

This has led me to the conclusion that it is God with whom I should speak first when I am concerned about a friend.

I hope it isn't just a habit of mine to have inner dialogues with people about what they might do to improve their situations. I have mentioned before that I have a secret inside bossy-pants, a rather strident character that is inclined to one-sided, inner conversations that begin with: "You know what you ought to do...? You ought to... blah, blah, blah..."

At some point, after the boss has been released, but before the obsessive guy with the megaphone starts barking, I try and remind myself to whom the other belongs. "Oh, that's right, he isn't mine, is he? He's yours," I say, as I turn to face the heavens.

There are moments when I almost feel the tug of this truth, as if two hands were gently placed on my cheeks, guiding my focus in this better direction.

If I am sincere in this transference of concern, I can sometimes be of use. If I honestly wish to be of service to this better angel of the friend's nature, I will be moved to speak when the time is right and speak gently.

In my early twenties, I had a friend for whom I acted as a sounding board. I believed that my utter silence would be beneficial when she began telling me her problems with her live-in boyfriend. As the months wore on, I heard more and more of the embarrassing details of her relationship with this young man. They were both sleeping around on each other, often with the other's good friends, and hurting each other terribly. I never said a word, just listened.

I would, however, go home to my new husband and vent about the days' discoveries. Adding, "If you ever dare to treat me as these two treat each other, I will walk out that door and never look back." Yet still, I went back for more, and still, I did not speak, and still, I brought my reaction home to my marriage.

One day I got a call from this friend who said that

her boyfriend had asked her to marry him and she had agreed. Apparently they were looking into purchasing health insurance and discovered that their policy would be cheaper if they were married.

"How romantic," I thought to myself, but still, I did not speak.

"You are my first call," she told me, "I know how much you love being married."

"Oh," I thought to myself, "I can think of so many juicy responses to that statement, I hardly know which to choose..." But still, I didn't choose, I didn't speak.

Eventually our friendship fell apart. It had to. One of us wasn't being honest. By my silence, I was practicing perfect complicity. I might as well have cheered them on with whistles and pompoms.

"Better to be a nettle in the side of your friend than his echo," writes Emerson.

You might ask why I never spoke my truth to this friend. At the time I thought her too fragile to hear it, and mistakenly believed I could prop up her delicate psyche with my silence. I thought she was mine to hold up.

As I age, I am more drawn to those who speak honestly to me. No matter how bitter the pill, no matter how long it takes to work.

I would rather hear a truth from a friend (and adjust my behavior accordingly) than meet the reactions of cold consequence which could be harsher. Maybe it's time to turn that old line from the prayer book around to read: "Speak now and try never to hold your peace."

Speak if you must, absolutely. Speak and then step back. Give room. They are God's to teach, God's to hold, God's to heal.

8

All God's Children

LATELY, WHENEVER I am feeling discouraged by the creepy-crawly progress of civilization, I try and imagine what a twenty-four-hour news cycle might have looked like in say... the Middle Ages. "After nineteen years of imprisonment, Mary Queen of Scots was beheaded this morning. Witnesses describe the scene as distressing, with the first blow of the executioner's ax just grazing the back of the head, the second landing on the neck but unable to separate the head from the body, and the third finally managing to pop the head cleanly away. Funeral arrangements are discouraged."

Or perhaps we might hear of a breaking news story from the Roman Empire in the year 73 BC. Senator

Crassus sent a strong message to rebels this morning when he ordered the crucifixion of six thousand slaves along the Appian Way leading into Rome. Visitors are encouraged to find alternative routes into the city.

Recently a woman I know was lamenting the political views of someone in her circle of friends and said, with utter exasperation, "She is just so … ignorant!" But ignorance, I thought to myself, true ignorance, seems to me neither a choice nor a sin. It merely indicates that the person has not yet received the grace of enlightenment, something that in most cases is very slow in coming. And furthermore, I suspect all of us harbor a degree of ignorance. Until we are able to see every single soul as our equal, we continue to hold onto a hint of backward thinking. Enlightenment is such a difficult achievement, if you can call it that, more like an improbable blossoming.

One thing that I am sure of is that this woman's unenlightened friend will not awaken as a result of anything her friend might say to her to try and pry her mind open. This is not a friend's part to play. This must happen by the grace of God working through the circumstances of her life, not by instruction, however friendly.

I find the stories of recovered white supremacists, or

"formers," as they call themselves, fascinating. Most will report that it was friendship, falling in love, and more important, the empathy shown to them when they didn't feel they deserved such a thing, that began to turn them away from extremism. It was not a sermon delivered by an enlightened acquaintance or just the right word spoken at the right time, it was love. One young man fell in love with a Jewish woman, another befriended a young Peruvian man in college, a third was given a job that had him visiting neighborhoods of kind brown people, communities that he had considered in his former life to be too dangerous to visit unarmed. These people opened their homes to him, and he was gently turned around by this show of kindness.

Some of the stories are quite dramatic, with those who had been swept up into the white supremacy movement suffering catastrophic loss: loss of love, loss of family, loss of freedom with years spent in prison. Others experienced gentler awakenings. I read of a man whose wife discovered one day that he was the principal contributor to one of the most heinous neo-Nazi websites for years during their marriage. She left him instantly. Some hearts are broken open, some gently pried. This man was to greatly regret his involvement in this hateful business. This seems to be the way God works. We must feel the circumstances of wrong behavior in order to turn away from it.

I know when faced with difficult circumstances, I have prayed for the difficulty to be taken away from me, lifted from me, but any good parent knows that this does not help the child become a man or a woman. We can be loved and supported through any difficulty, but it is not a truly loving act to remove a lesson entirely.

A friend's teenage son, along with a group of boys from his hometown, landed into trouble with the law many years ago. One of the boys was the son of a local judge and this father was determined to drop the charges against all of the boys, when my friend wrote a strong letter of complaint. She demanded that her son be treated like any other young citizen of their community. Her argument was that a message of favoritism would be ruinous to these boys. I never heard the end of this story but was struck by the wisdom of the parent.

A good parent will try and love the unconscious child through the process of being made conscious. This is what we should be able to expect from our parents. If a parent lifts the child onto his shoulders, stepping over the lesson in the way, the child will never reach consciousness.

Oh, and the list of potential recipients of enlightenment is endless. I do not envy the Creator the job of cracking open his hard-shelled creatures. And nothing so calcifies our crusty selves as isolationism and hate. It builds up and blocks the light from shining into our soul windows. Of course, it's easy to see in a white supremacist that the ears and eyes and heart have been hardened by anger, and many have inherited their furious views from their parents, making their crust generational, causing the hard shell to become much more difficult to shatter.

I would suggest that we all have a touch of isolationism in us. It might be more difficult to identify in some of us. It could be an intolerance of the ignorant, a sense that one's family is better than another's, it could be a well-disguised disdain for people from a particular part of the world. Most of us have subtle cultural biases that haunt us: men with women, women with men, atheists with the religious, the religious with those who do not practice a faith, white with brown, brown with white, white with narrow-minded white, young with old, old with young. Just dig down into anyone's psyche and you will uncover a perceived inferior. And feelings of superiority are not far from viewing another as an enemy.

Jesus suggested that we love our enemies. I have been

trying to determine whether this was an utterly new concept for mankind when he offered this challenge. Surely it was a revolutionary thought in a culture that practiced the law of an eye for an eye and a tooth for a tooth. Did anyone else expect this much of us? The Buddha suggested that one could find freedom from envy and hate through the practice of nonattachment, but did he specifically say that we were to love our enemies? This seems to require an effort on our part. Love is an outpouring. Nonattachment is a releasing. Jesus came to suggest that we pour love out of our hearts and onto those whom we hated. I'm just sayin'...

I suspect that until we are able to perform this nearly impossible feat, we have not thrown the doors of our souls open quite as wide as they will go. Some of our spirit still stands in shadow.

March on, good soldiers...

9

Wishes

Many years ago, I got it in my head that I would like to visit the redwoods. I had been among these great beings before. The last time was in the Muir Woods outside of San Francisco. That was a lovely encounter, but I was thinking that I would like a more private meeting, something very intimate. So, for a time, whenever I met anyone who lived in or had visited California extensively, I would ask, "Do you know of any unpopular redwood forests in the state, somewhere I might hope to be alone with the grand old giants?"

I never did receive a very clear answer and forgot the desire entirely by the time I booked my husband and myself a week's vacation on the coast of Southern Oregon. We spent each day hiking the state's Douglas fir forests, stunning walks, often punctuated by dramatic views of the Pacific Ocean. One night we met a couple staying in the same inn as ours. They had driven up from the south and mentioned that they had made a stop at the Jedediah Smith State Park in Northern California. "It's well worth the trip," they told us, "Only an hour from here. Make sure you visit the really old guys at Stout Grove."

We planned our visit for the next day. The park was marked like a faded treasure map. Enigmatic, you might call it. We immediately got lost—drove forever on a wildly churned-up dirt road—passed Stout Grove—decided to push on to a more private place—turned around when the road became absurdly rutted—and found ourselves back at Stout Grove. There were perhaps eight cars parked on the side of the road (which was the most-visited spot in the park), and their owners looked as if they were planning on remaining among the stout ones for a little while, and then making their way back to civilization. Their flimsy footwear gave them away.

Matt and I, however, hoped to hike, and after visiting the grove, we went in search of the trail that, according to our map, would lead us through the redwoods along a creek bed for what looked like many miles of backcountry hiking.

We found the trailhead with some difficulty and followed it for just a few minutes before it abruptly ended at a stream. We were about to turn around in frustration when a man walked up to us. He was certainly not telegraphing an intention to hike. He wore flip-flops and strolled along with a couple of drowsy teenagers. He was an old hippy, tie-dyed, with flowing locks. This clearly endeared him to my husband, for, like many men, Matt is loath to ask for directions. In fact, I don't believe he did ask for help, but the man offered us his knowledge of the area.

"I used to come here as a child," he said, "and there was, I believe, a bridge over this stream, right here, with the trail picking up on the other side. If you are willing to take your shoes off and wade through the creek, I think you will find the path, just there," he said, pointing to a spot on the other shore.

We followed his advice and set out on what proved to be one of the most magical walks we have ever taken. We passed two other hikers, otherwise the only inhabitants of this forest were a huge chorus of enormous lady and gentleman redwoods, singing their hymns of hushed silence. At one point, feeling a little overheated, we scrambled down to the creek, stripped off our clothes, and took a dip, assured that the only ones looking were an elegant company of piney titans.

It wasn't until many days later that I realized that a long-held wish had been granted to me. And even though I had forgotten the request, the heavens clearly had not.

I wonder how often a wish of mine has been granted without my acknowledgment. I shudder to think. I hope I have not been so cavalier with any of my answered prayers.

The difference, it seems to me, between a wish and a prayer might be discovered in its aftermath. With an answered prayer one is more inclined to look up and say, "Thank you,"—at least that would seem the fitting response to having a prayer answered—whereas an answered wish is often accepted without acknowledgment. But otherwise, I imagine that both wishes and prayers are heard by the same good father, and the gift of an answer always cries out for gratitude.

I have a friend who lost her husband, and two years later decided to sell her house. She eventually received a nice offer, but her fear was that the two outdoor, feral cats that she and her husband had fed for years, would not meet with the same hospitality from their buyers. I am sure she hoped for a happy result, but she probably did not pray for it, though I don't know that for sure. She certainly wished for it. The good news is that when the new owners took over the house, not only did they look after the cats, but they made them special beds in an enclosure out of the wind and continue to discover ways to fuss over them.

"Anything large enough for a wish to light upon, is large enough to hang a prayer upon," writes George MacDonald.

I understand that many people have a hard time believing that God cares for our small prayers. Take the image of a football player publicly crossing himself before a game. I would say that the prayer to be spared from crippling, or even fatal injury is no small item, but more to the point, who are we to size up another man's prayer? Isn't this up to the one to whom he prays?

It seems to me that we can justify praying over a hangnail, if we remember to be mindful of the one to whom we pray and thankful for the answer.

George MacDonald continues from the previous quote: "For the real good of every gift it is essential, first, that the giver be in the gift—as God always is, for he is love—and next, that the receiver know and receive the giver in the gift."

I have been given small gifts, kitchen utensils for instance, that remind me of the person who gave them to me every time I pick them up. I have a garlic press that always has me thinking of my brother-in-law, Paul, whenever I use it. In fact, I recently had to replace it after many years of use, and still remember that the original was given to us by Paul.

I have only just recently begun to see flowers as clear gifts from the heavens. No other earthly animal can appreciate a flower as a human can. Certain flowers are tasty to some animals, but only man can value them aesthetically. Flowers seem distinctly created for our enjoyment. They seem almost frivolous gifts from the Great Creator, sent specifically to lift our spirits. But how often is it that I think of the Giver when I see a flower? I am ashamed to say.

How patient this God of ours is, willing to wait epochs of time for our acknowledgment. Might as well start today. "That is an extraordinarily pleasing little dandelion, thank you Dear One! Oh, and however you orchestrated that visit to the unpopular redwood forest, I will never know, but how thoughtful of you! I so loved that gift."

10

Paper Snowflakes

I AM READING a book about the sneaky mach-inations of the ego, and how easy it is to fall for its cunning ways. If I were caught with the book on camera, viewers might witness the knowing smile, the little pepperings of "ah-ha" moments, the bursts of "amen brother."

The author warns against falling into the well-occupied traps of the little bugger: our vanities, perceived injuries, unchecked ambitions. This last one is where my ears perk up. He points to all of the wisdom, both current and ancient, that suggests that the only path to happiness must take us through the dark woods of ego annihilation. I sooooooooo agree.

And yet I feel it's my duty to confess, the moment I

put the book down, my ego goes back to dreamin' and schemin'.

There have been times when I wished I had been born with absolutely no ambitious goals, no drive, desire to create, to reach an audience. But then it occurs to me that the man who wrote this wise book had to have mustered a degree of "look what I've got," in order to get his book published.

Most of us are loath to toot our own horns. The majority would prefer to be plucked out of the throng, set up with all sorts of support (cash and careful handling), to expedite the delivery of their gifts among the greater population: those hungry ones, eager to consume our clever ways with words, paint, organization, song, political genius, leadership. When in fact, it might be better for our egos to be forced to search out ways to find an audience ourselves, more humbling.

The ego bloats when we believe these gifts make us more special than others. The reason they are called gifts is that we were given them. In fact, there are undoubtedly millions of others with a similar gift. Skill is another matter. That we work for. But gifts are different. Webster's College Dictionary defines a gift as "something bestowed or acquired without being sought or earned by the receiver." All of us, in short, are gifted.

Love is a gift. And all of us are gifted with love.

If we really saw our gifts as gifts, there would be little self-conceit in giving them away. The act of finding patrons, audience, homes in which to hang our paintings, eyes to read our books would be more like a child, singing a song to her mother, a kindergartener bringing home a crepe paper snowflake for his father. "Look what I made for you!"

A preschooler isn't thinking, "wow, wow, I must be pretty good at this, huh."

She isn't planning her future as the darling of the art world, mentally dressing herself in striking outfits and arresting hats. He isn't practicing serious facial expressions and wistful poses.

When I was six or so I made a brief appearance on a local television show in Louisville, Kentucky called *T Bar V Ranch Time*. I don't remember anything about the day we filmed but will never forget the subsequent horror of watching myself when the show aired. Apparently, I thought it might add a touch of sophistication if I adopted a careless bend to my left wrist—I must have seen the affectation on a movie star or a model. It seemed that once I made this reckless decision, I felt I could not retract it without shattering the illusion of refinement, and so held my arm in this position the entire show (which seemed a tortured eternity!) It was my first lesson in the absurdity of striking a pose, a lesson that has returned and returned in many faintly disguised ways.

There is a moment in everyone's history, somewhere between the age of five and nine, when he or she becomes self-aware. As heartbreaking it is to see a child lose his innate comfort with himself, this is a necessary step toward maturity. The good news is, at some point in the lives of many of us, after we have tried out hundreds of uncomfortable postures, assumed all sorts of unnecessary roles, when we begin to long for our old, true selves. Typically this yearning will arise sometime in middle age, after our awkward courtship-and-job-interview years and before our ancient ones.

One can hear the rumblings of the original self among this aging population, "I'm just too old to get swept up into that kind of drama." You hear, "I simply cannot pretend anymore that I am thrilled with these gatherings."

These little truths add up and eventually hold the power to expose our authentic selves. I am not suggesting that one's preferences should constantly be made public. We have all known the trying personality that is bent on announcing to anyone who will listen their fierce likes and dislikes. On the whole, if we are comfortable with ourselves, we won't feel the need to announce our partialities. We will hold these lightly and, unless we are at immediate risk of being poisoned or hit by a bus, we will hold them silently.

The point is to begin to speak the little truths to ourselves. If we train ourselves to see the little truths, this will help us to identify greater and greater ones, which will eventually lead us to understand the great truth behind the workings of the world.

The longer we are on earth, the more opportunities we have to discover that we are all essentially on the same journey, each of us capable of all things human. Our egos, propped up by our dissimilarities, begin to slowly melt away as we learn, one humiliation at a time, that however enlightened we think we are, each of us is, as Emerson suggests, "a god in ruin." Hopefully, after many years on planet earth, we will gather enough humility until it no longer pains us, when we hear of a neighbor's shortcoming, to look for its counterpart in ourselves.

This is what I believe true ego annihilation means: the willingness to join the human race with all of its failings, to love our ordinariness, to honor the good and common, and despise the stingy and arrogant in all natures, especially our own.

So yes, let us continue to strive to send our gifts out into the world, whatever they are, knowing that every offering, whether it's a smile or a symphony, is just one more paper snowflake offered in grateful appreciation of life on this planet.

11

Pilgrimage

I WENT ON a pilgrimage lately, though I didn't recognize it at the time.

I have rarely experienced any sort of epiphany while traveling. God seems to prefer that our meetings take place along my familiar paths. Knowing this, I have followed the same looping path through the woods near my home for 28 years.

It isn't for lack of travel and trying that I have come to this conclusion. I have visited many an ancient, holy place, but never, from the magnitude of St. Paul's Cathedral in Rome to the mountains of Machu Picchu, have I felt more than a tourist.

The other weekend I went to a conference presented by the Marion Institute in Massachusetts with the British author and publisher Mark Booth. The talk revolved around European female mystics over the centuries and featured a special interview with the modern Irish mystic Lorna Byrne. Lorna claims to have been seeing the spiritual world within the physical since she was a child. She is able to see angels and departed spirits as you and I see one another. I have been reading her books and handing them to friends for years.

Lorna Byrne is a soft-spoken woman in her early sixties, who wrestled with such profound learning disabilities when young that she was left barely able to read. She speaks her books into a recording device and a friend transcribes them. She is uncomfortable with the attention that has been stirred up by her revelations and hides her face behind her hands when applauded. She makes no extraordinary claims to be able to heal or awaken, she denies that she is closer to God than you or I. She simply tells her story, which illuminates the amount of divine aid available to us. If only we could see through her eyes, she tells us, we would see that we are always surrounded by the angelic kingdom, with its army of "unemployed angels," a term she uses to describe those beings who surround us and yearn to be allowed to assist us. The only power that she claims for herself is the power of prayer, which each of us possesses. Her advice always is to ask for help, for ourselves, our neighbors, our planet. No prayer goes unheeded, she confirms. When asked the rules for prayer, she assures us that God isn't interested in rules. When asked about judgment, about right and wrong, she assures us that God is love.

At the end of the day's talk, we lined up for one of Lorna's blessings. Lorna has said that something special is allowed to occur during these blessings, but she does not wish to reveal what this is. She has written the information and sealed it in an envelope to be opened after her death. Clearly, Lorna fears celebrity. And, having been in her presence several times, I fear it for her. If she were any less pure, I doubt she would be able to hold onto her gifts.

Over a hundred of us lined up, as if in church, to be blessed by Lorna. She laid her hands on our heads and moved through the quiet gathering, one by one. I have always loved having my head held, ever since a child when my mother would rest her hand on my head. That much was naturally sweet to me, but it wasn't until I moved away from the others, that I felt it. Something entered my heart, plop, something like gold, or like light, difficult to identify, but something felt.

For many years I have understood that joy is an inside

job, that the world does not hold the key to contentment or bliss. Or rather, that something must be alight inside of me for the light to reach the world around me. I have understood that the life I experience is colored by my attitude. Like wearing a pair of sunglasses, according to the strength of the glasses, the world will appear either dimmed by darkness or flooded by light.

Perhaps half of my life, I saw the world through what I can now see were the glasses of disappointment. I believe I was tempted to pick them up after my early years of being a bottom-of-the-barrel student and was further prompted by two particularly miserable years in a loveless performing arts school. By the time I was out in the world trying to find work in my chosen field, I couldn't see without the glasses of disappointment and expected to fail at every turn. Or perhaps I should say that I expected the world to fail me. It did, naturally.

The Franciscan priest Richard Rohr, in his book *Falling Upward*, assures us that the world must fail us in order for us to find the kingdom.

"If we try to make the Church into the Kingdom of God," he writes," "we create a false idol that will disappoint us. If we try to make the world itself into the Kingdom, we will always be resentful when it does not come through." Rohr goes on to warn us not to wait until after death for the Kingdom, but to seek it in the present.

If I had to guess what is written in that mysterious envelope of Lorna Byrne's, I would say it had to do with the delivery of a small drop of connection or, looked at another way, the ignition of the spark of God inside each of us, lighting up the kingdom within.

I suspect that many, like me, will pay the idea of an inner Kingdom lip service for years before it really comes home. We will repeat our platitudes, "Happiness is an inside job. Change your attitude and the world changes around you." All very fine until you feel it. All very well until you very slowly begin to live from this notion.

Several days after I came home from my pilgrimage, and while I was on my morning walk through the woods, I became aware that instead of my typical beggy sorts of prayers, my daily supplications for help delivered to a random place somewhere over my head, my focus had shifted. Instead of struggling to be heard, I was releasing, quieting my spirit in order to locate the place where I and the one to whom I prayed were united.

I am reminded of the revelations of Lady Julian of Norwich from the fourteenth century, where she is given a series of divine visions. I refer specifically to her use of the word "one-ing," a term she employs to explain the process of the soul being knit together with God.

"Prayer ones the soul to God" she wrote, "Prayer becomes a witness that the soul wills as God wills."

I felt one-ed and have felt one-ed ever since.

If this is the gift of the blessing, dear Lorna, then I am eternally grateful. May its comfort ripple through all hearts around the world. May its peace rest in everyone.

Amen.

12

A Measure of Meaning

Viktor Frankl, in the book *Man's Search for Meaning* (his account of the four years he was imprisoned in the Nazi death camps during the second world war), suggests that there are three ways in which man can find meaning in life: by the work that he does, by the people he loves, and finally by the meaning to be discovered in unavoidable suffering.

Frankl understood that, though there was no meaning behind the horrors of torture and extermination in the camps, no meaning to the practice of starvation and humiliation, there was always a choice offered him as he made his way through each day. Each moment gave him an opportunity to act with an open or a stingy-hearted response. In every encounter with a fellow prisoner, he could either turn away or offer comfort. With every encounter with those who imprisoned him, he could either choose to react with offense or detachment. Meaning, therefore, had to do with the choice he made in each moment. In a broader sense, what Dr. Frankl concluded is that amid the experiences of a man's life, exists a purpose of individual meaning, discovered by our daily choices.

Only one out of twenty-eight people who entered the camps survived, and one of the reasons that Viktor believes that he lived was that he had been writing a book before he entered the camps, one that he thought could be of help to the field of psychiatry, and those suffering from mental illness. Viktor had been a young psychiatrist in Vienna when he was taken. And, even though that manuscript had been confiscated and destroyed when he entered the first camp, he still carried the thoughts in his head. These thoughts, he believed, were worth living for.

When he returned to Vienna, he discovered that his young, pregnant wife had starved in the camps, his parents had been gassed and his beloved city bombed to ruins. He might have been tempted to take his life on his return but he still held the book in his head. He wrote the book, shared it with friends, and one of his friends suggested that he also write a book about his time in the camps. Viktor entered a bombed-out room in his city and didn't emerge for nine days, having completed *Man's Search for Meaning*.

He became an internationally respected voice in his field, affecting millions and millions of lives. I would count myself among that number. Reading his book has stretched my mind in extraordinary ways, the results of which I am still uncovering.

In *Man's Search for Meaning* Frankl writes of coming to the United States and setting up a psychiatric practice, after having practiced in Europe for several years after the war. He refers to something that he found among the youth in the US, which he said existed in Europe, but was much more prevalent in the States. This was a syndrome that he called "Existential Vacuum." He suspected that this was a result of the children in the States having so much provided for them, without any effort on their part. He came to see that this could lead to their feeling purposeless, unnecessary. It is difficult to feel such a thing as Existential Vacuum when you have a list of farm chores to complete. The modern middle-class household in the mid-twentieth century when Viktor was practicing provided a sort of breeding ground for this feeling of worthlessness. I can absolutely relate to this diagnosis of Existential Vacuum. I believe I had it in spades.

When I was growing up in Louisville, Kentucky in the sixties, our family hired a woman to care for the house and a man to care for the yard. I wasn't even required to make my bed when I was young. I never pulled a weed, planted a seed, was never invited to help with a meal (all chores from which I gather great satisfaction today) and, as a result, I wrestled with the haunting feeling of being without value. I felt this for many years. Honestly, until I began to write in my early thirties, I lived with the vague feeling of being redundant. By this time I had taught myself how to care for a home, to cook, to pull a weed, but it was taking pen to paper that seemed to answer this emptiness more completely than any other activity. This is still the case. I will add that it isn't just writing that seems to banish the vacuum but writing something that I believe might have the power to slightly lift my reading friend to a place where she might see a situation from a different angle, where he might have a truth exposed that had always existed inside of him, but which was until now obscured. And, it isn't always writing for Listen Well or a book that I am working on, but could be a letter or even an email.

In his essay, "On the Meaning and Value of Life,"

Viktor Frankl writes, "Life itself means being questioned, means answering." And he goes on to say about the discovery of meaning, "Life no longer appears to us as a given, but as something given over to us."

That might take a moment to digest. I think I see what he means.

When life is a given, it feels like primary school to a child in the US. Every child is expected to attend some sort of school, and the child might feel trapped by the system, and be tempted to trudge through, bored, and watching the clock. When life is given over to you, it is more like the opportunity to attend school for a child in Haiti, where education is not necessarily a given, but an opportunity, and one that could have a significant effect on the child's future life.

When life has meaning, we embrace and engage our learning, study our choices, and try and respond thoughtfully. Without meaning, we trudge through, holding our breath, until the bell rings.

In the camps, Frankl's life had been reduced to something almost inhuman, a number, which was not even considered worth counting. The prisoners were routinely told that they weren't worth the paltry, watered-down bowl of soup that they were provided once a day. But, Viktor maintains that he still valued his life because he held the power of deciding how he would respond to even the smallest of choices. This is where he found meaning.

Looked at this way, life, it seems, is a collection of small, but significant questions. I say significant because to passively refuse to make any choice is a sort of mini death, it is the denial of an opportunity to discover meaning. Some choices are immediately revelatory, they will cause you joy or shame. Others are more like planting a bulb in autumn so that it will come up in the spring. You can't necessarily see the result, but you can believe in its blossoming.

Every day, therefore, holds an opportunity to parse out a measure of meaning and to embrace the gift of life.

13

To Keep the Sabbath

IN THE Gospel of Thomas, one of the recently discovered Gnostic gospels, Jesus is quoted as saying, "If you do not keep the Sabbath as a Sabbath you will never see the Father." The line that precedes this is "If you do not fast from the world you will not find the Kingdom."

Interesting that this rebellious voice, of one who came to shake up the rigid dogma of the Jewish tradition, would be stressing the need for fasting and keeping the Sabbath.

We live in a culture that has lost sight of the importance of preserving one day a week for laying down the things of the world and focusing on the spiritual. Of course, many still do practice this wise counsel, but all day long? I do not wish to imply that I know how to manage a full day of divine focus, but after reading this line in Thomas's gospel, I thought I would like to at least try.

I chose a recent Sunday to begin.

I had nothing scheduled that day and was alone. This was helpful, of course. There was no one but me to get in my way, but then I cast a rather large shadow on myself, being so close and all.

I decided to begin the ritual on my daily walk in the woods. This, I thought, would give me a head start, as my walk could be seen as an hour and a half long mini-Sabbath. The problem is I don't always fast from the world, so to speak, on these walks and waste all sorts of time babbling to myself. But lately, I had been launching a campaign against my inner chatterbox.

I take my morning walk in a neighboring rural park. When I arrive at the parking area, I step out of the car, open the back door where my two dogs are straining to be on their way, snap on their leashes, and lead them across a dirt road and onto a wooded path. After about fifty feet I release the dogs and send up my first prayer, that they will not scurry back to the parking lot to eat trash. At this point, I begin my exercise of prayer and contemplation. On most days this practice consists of faint attempts at prayer, interrupted by dashes out to worry over some troublesome thought, followed by a return to feeble prayer, interrupted by a mad foray around the neighborhood to think of ways my neighbors might improve their lives, followed contritely by prayers for my neighbors, interrupted by bursts of alarm about some nagging personal anxiety before I turn back in abject shame to prayer.

In an effort to still this frantic activity, I had recently decided to refrain from any prayers whatsoever on my walk, but to save them for other times during my day. I wished to remain silent and present, allowing my ears to open, eyes to notice, mind to still.

After several days of this practice (for which I must admit, if I had been graded, I would have deserved a mark no higher than D-), I stepped out of my car in the parking lot one morning and at my feet saw a tiny torn piece of trash from some unrecognizable package, with the words *ZIP IT* on it.

"Mmm…." I mumbled, pulling an imaginary zipper across my lips.

I came very near to getting a B+ that day.

But this is as far as I had gotten with my practice of silence and attention when I tried to keep the Sabbath for an entire day. Like signing up for a triathlon for next Tuesday, it was a tad ambitious.

I began that Sunday morning, as I do every day, pulling into the parking lot and walking my quiet loop through the woods. I didn't grade myself this time, but I didn't anticipate earning any awards for contemplation. The difference on this day was that I tried very hard not to dictate what would come next. I was leaving it up to the good angels of the Sabbath.

In short, I noodled. I noodled around the house and at one point thought I might noodle back out for a walk without my madcap dogs. It was spring and there were all sorts of baby animals out there who were naturally shy around my little terrors. I had just that week noted that I had not yet witnessed my first fawn of the season.

I will never get used to the fact that I live in a place that has such an intimate relationship with the deer. This is an extraordinarily beautiful creature, and I marvel at its loveliness every day. There are those in my neighborhood who see our deer as garden-eating nuisances. I have watched a nursing doe eating fresh roses from off my bushes, and yet still loved her. The rare sighting of a deer's newborn is almost more joy than my heart can bear, like a basket of kittens or a hummingbird's nest.

On my appointed Sabbath, in the late morning, I thought I would walk through our neighboring farmland rather than return to the woods. I cut out aimlessly across the fields, always noodling, like a two-month-old puppy, never traveling in a straight line, stopping to sniff everything, chat with a couple of women on horseback, noodle some more, look at the view, noodle, notice, noodle, sniff, noodle, prick up my ears and stare again, noodle, noodle, inspect a wildflower, noodle, noodle, noodle, sit.

I had only been seated for a few minutes in a little stand of trees at the edge of a field when a fawn, looking to be about three weeks old, tripped by just about fifteen feet from me. This would have been gift enough, had not another tiny newborn fawn popped up from the brush very near me to call to the older fawn. The tiny one nuzzled the older one, and even for a confused moment attempted to nurse from it. If the older fawn could have giggled, he might have sounded a bit like a Disney character. He played and nuzzled and frolicked around the little baby for a few moments, while I sat frozen with ecstatic attention in my place among the trees. Eventually the older fawn decided to continue on his way, and the newborn attempted to follow, taking several difficult steps. The older fawn turned to address the tiny one with a parting nod and then sprang effortlessly away, leaving the little darling to sway and stagger back to his nursery very near to me in the woods. He dutifully tucked himself back in his makeshift bed to wait for his mama. I sat with him for a little while longer, drinking him in with my eyes, before deciding it best to make myself scarce so that the Mama would not be shy to return.

I walked home as if from a first kiss, dreamy, grateful. "I have seen the Father today." I thought in happy Sabbath wonder, "I have caught a glimpse of the Kingdom."

14 ✿

Small Miracles

I HAVE A story for the Miracle of the Month Club. That is, if I ever start such a thing, which is unlikely, as I am not much of a club person. Though, I do love to share tales of the miraculous. Perhaps if I continue to share my small yarns of the miraculous, those who enjoy these stories will consider writing to share with me their own precious, sparkly accounts. I suppose together we could be viewed as a sort of club.

Here is my most recent tale...

I had to make a call the other day to our trash removal company to ask them to deliver a recycle bin to our home. I called the number and was handed off to a woman in Texas—ours is a national company—and began to explain that my husband had put in an order for a receptacle for our recyclables quite some time ago, but that it had never arrived. The woman said that she would begin another order request, but that I would have to bear with her while she dove into her computer to set up delivery, at which point we both grew silent. After a moment I thought to myself, this woman seems like a good egg, I think I would like to bless her. I closed my eyes and imagined that my hand was patting her on the head, as I asked the heavens for a blessing for her. Two seconds passed before she began to tell me her life story. "I have to get out of Texas one of these days, "she began. "I'm taking care of my ninety-six-year-old aunt, and I always say to her that when she dies, I'm going to leave this state." I held my breath, waiting for more. "I tried to get out once," she continued. "I got on a bus years ago with my kids, and we rode and rode, but we never managed to get out of Texas."

At this point I laughed, adding, "well, maybe that's why those of us in the rest of the country don't meet many people from Texas, so few manage to escape."

The conversation went on like this for a while, before we wrapped up our session and went on about the business of our day.

I must remember to send out a blessing when I am

hoping that the person to whom I am speaking will open up with me and share themselves.

When I lived in New York City and had to take a taxi somewhere, I would often ask the heavens for the type of person that I would like to have as a driver. Sometimes I wanted someone really kind. Occasionally I needed someone zippy, a no-nonsense, pedal-to-the-metal sort. But most of the time I wanted a peaceful, gentle ride with someone who would share something of themselves with me: their story or some wisdom they had learned along the way. More often than not, the supplication was answered in perfect order. One time, on my way to the corner to hail a ride out to LaGuardia Airport, feeling a bit anxious about leaving home, I asked for someone who would make me feel safe, someone who would calm my rattled nerves. The man who picked me up, I was to discover within the first few minutes, had been a county judge in a small town in Michigan for many years, and was retired and living in Brooklyn. He needed a little extra cash and so drove a few hours a week. We talked during the entire ride out to the airport. His driving style was as even as his temperament and I felt as safe as a babe in her mother's arms. The feeling lasted throughout my travels that day.

Sometimes the rules to life can appear so simple. Oh,

and then there are other times, complex times, times when the answers to our requests are like opening a paint can with our teeth. I will not be dealing with that sort of story today, only the small, unassuming ones.

A while ago, I read a narrative by a woman who had had a brush with death and claimed to have met God. Many who return from the other side will make such assertions, though the form in which this grand being presents itself varies. I cannot remember the details of the appearance of the Great Spirit, but I do remember one phrase that this woman took away from her experience. It was a suggestion. "Imagine," God said to her, "if it was just you and me." When I read those words I thought, "Hm, I am sensing a profound truth here, which I must take some time to absorb."

The obvious conclusion is that God is in everything, every human, every bird, beast, tree, rock. The great masters have been trying to help us to understand this concept for centuries. The not-so-obvious conclusion is that we are in a constant state of relationship with all that surrounds us, with all of life. From the moment we wake to the moment we fall asleep, we are in fellowship with the Everything and the All, for God is in everything and in all.

Furthermore, I must presume, God is not only in

everything but is the connective tissue between everything. Remember the woman on the phone from the waste management company? I asked for her blessing, which is to say that I asked that God might bless her. This connected us, put us in relationship with one another. There was no distance between us because everything between us was God.

It seems to me that if this is a truth, then this Great Loving Spirit must long to hear from us, therefore I assume that even if we make a tiny taxi-driver request, this is at least an effort toward communication, and will be sweet music to the heavens.

Many of my friends, when I share one of my small testaments to the miraculous, will say to me, "Well, that sort of thing happens to you, Margaret, but never to me." I don't believe this for a minute. Why would the heavens choose to communicate more with one person than another? Perhaps the secret to this interaction lies in God's suggestion to the woman who had the near-death experience. "Imagine if it was just you and me."

The simple conclusion is: ask. Maybe those who tell me that they do not experience the daily answers that I speak of, who believe their lives are less full of magic than mine, are simply being polite. Perhaps they feel a certain embarrassment around asking for smallish things. I understand. But perhaps by asking for answers to our modest desires we are being trained to rely on God to answer our grand and weighty ones. A child who keeps the line of communication open to her parent will not hesitate to get in touch, and this attitude could very well save her life one day.

These mornings, when I wake, and before I open my eyes, I will think, "Good morning, Dear One. I wonder what you might have up your sleeve for me today. But, before we get going, I have a few people that I'd like for you to bless." I think of those I am most concerned about. Pat, pat, pat, I imagine my hand on the heads of those I am concerned about. Pat, pat, pat, pat. I move on to the next one. Pat, pat, pat. I continue through my list. Pat, pat. "There... Thank you, dear."

15

Lifting the Veil

I HAVE ALWAYS loved to tell stories. They have always held the power to awaken me where scholarly outlines or how-to presentations fall short.

I especially like stories that point to the continuation of the soul after death. These can take many forms: dream visits from departed souls, the sense when awake that one is being visited by a departed loved one, near-death stories, unusual animal sightings around a passing. Sometimes I will share these stories when I am not entirely sure of the philosophy of the person with whom I am speaking and will slap my head afterward in mortified disbelief at my big mouth.

I have two fears: that my tale might come across as implausibly daffy and cause the listener to harden in his materialistic view, or that I might appear too sure, too glibly confident of an afterlife, and therefore not respectful of this life, or worse, insensitive to the effects that death might have on those who remain behind.

I once told a cousin of mine who was dying of pancreatic cancer that he might look forward to seeing my grandmother, his aunt, who had loved him fiercely. "Aunty Jane will take great delight in having you with her."

He answered with sharp precision. "No. This is the only life. I'm sure of that. I have had a good one. I have done what I wished to do, designed the houses I wished to build (he was an architect), met the people I would have wanted to meet, and I am tired. I'm ready for life to be over."

I felt a chill travel up my spine. I promptly shut my mouth and the conversation dwindled to an end. He died soon after. After our talk I was haunted by my audacity, fearing that my cousin might have been stung by what he could have viewed as a tactless attempt at false hope. I felt this for months afterward, until I had my dream. In the dream my cousin and I were sitting on a deserted beach, one that we had visited together when he was alive. At some point, we decided to go into the water and bodysurf in the waves. I dove in and began to flip around in the surf, diving down and popping up to the surface, and eventually hovering and waiting for a wave large enough to carry me into the shore. I looked over to locate my cousin and discovered that he was already busy riding the waves, but instead of lying flat and swimming, he was able to ride on top of the surface, on the soles of his feet. Like a surfer without a board, he took the waves in perfect tightrope balance, hopping off the wave with ease when it crashed into the shore. He performed this remarkable feat again and again, like a ten-year-old with a new trick, wearing an expression of exuberant joy. I watched for a moment and then snapped awake.

When I woke from this dream, I had the sure understanding that it was a visitation. I felt my cousin's desire to let me know that I had not offended him, and I was able to release my cringing embarrassment about our telephone conversation.

Very recently I spoke to a friend whose husband had passed through the Great Door. He had made his transition only two days earlier and my friend was naturally extremely tender. At one point in our conversation, she told me a story that had happened around the time of his death.

One of the roles that her husband had performed

in their years together was that of official locater of her reading glasses, items that I gather she misplaced weekly. She had recently purchased a handsome pair with red frames, of which she was particularly fond. In the final days in the hospital, as her husband struggled between life and death, she was asked to fill out numerous hospital forms, and it seemed that no matter how many times she went hunting around in her purse for her glasses, they were nowhere to be found. In one of her husband's waking moments, she mentioned that she could not find her favorite reading glasses, and he comforted her, assuring her that she would find them. "They're not lost," he said, "They will turn up. I promise." In the middle of that night after she had returned home, he died.

The next day, there was an even greater need for the glasses to help her deal with the paperwork required around death. My friend went on a mad search in her home for her glasses again, without success, and eventually had to return to the hospital without them. At the hospital, having been handed a fresh pile of forms to fill out, she took one last dive into her purse, and there were her glasses, nestled within easy access, as if her husband had spent the night searching for them and had placed them carefully in her bag.

"He found my glasses! I know it was him." She said to me, "I know it! I felt him with me!" She paused before she continued. "I wouldn't share this story with everyone, Margaret," she told me, "but I know how you feel about these things."

I have to say this was one of my proudest moments. To be known as someone with whom one might feel safe sharing one's story of miraculous connection made all of my previous fears about a negative response melt away.

"I understand," I told her. "Some might react with an embarrassed, 'Well, of course he lives on in your heart.' And, you want to respond, 'Yes, yes, of course he does, but he also visits!'"

This story would seem to champion a habit of open communication about such subjects.

In the book *Letters by a Modern Mystic*, by Frank C. Laubach, a collection of letters written from a son to his father in the 1930s while working as a missionary in the Philippine Islands, the author writes...

"I may say that it seems to me that we really seldom do anybody much good except as we share the deepest experiences of our souls... It is not the fashion to tell your inmost thoughts, but there are many wrong fashions, and concealment of the best in us is wrong. I disapprove of the usual practice of talking "small talk" whenever we meet, and holding a veil over our souls. ... I hunger for others to tell me their soul adventures."

Oh gosh, I so agree, but the embarrassment! It can be so humiliating to share the miraculous with the close-minded.

All the more reason to persevere, I suppose. Often our bravest acts are those when we chance looking like a fool in order to give comfort. And we never know when a story, once discarded as nonsense, might come back around to offer solace.

Be brave, my brothers and sisters. Lift the veil for one another.

16 ✿

Pyramid Scheme

I READ OF a woman who said that when she was a child, she was given two clear messages from the heavens. I am not sure how they were delivered. One was that love was the answer to all of the world's problems. The other was that the world was upside down because we valued power and privilege over love.

Picture a pyramid, its base on Earth, with the pinnacle pointing to the sky. This is how too many of us have viewed the progress of mankind. The object of life in this system is to work hard enough to raise yourself to as close to the top as you can manage. The higher one rises within this structure, the less one serves others, and the more one is served. If you are fortunate enough to reach the top, you are served by everyone, and you serve no one.

This could be seen as the Great Pyramid Scheme.

All of the world's wisdom teachers have said just the opposite: essentially, that it is in service to our fellow man that we find meaning, that until you find your service you will feel empty, lost. This service could be as simple as the practice of small kindnesses, or as grand as the invention of the light bulb, but the idea of struggling to get to a point where one no longer needs to serve is all backwards. Why would one strive to be unnecessary?

This reminds me of those who work furiously to retire early and go quietly mad because they no longer feel useful, or those expatriates who move to beautiful places like Costa Rica, to be done with the struggle of the developed world and live off of beauty, and end up drinking themselves to death. You can't live off of scenery.

I read a story of a woman who had a brush with death and while visiting the other side, met a spirit whom she understood to be her spiritual teacher. This man, whom she had never known in life, had been a truck driver during his time on Earth and was specifically chosen to teach this woman humility. What better employment for an active inner life than one requiring hours of driving? I imagine that not many of us on the path to awakening would look for our teachers in passing semis, but therein lies the upside-downness of our thinking.

When I was young, being raised in Louisville, Kentucky in the fifties and sixties, most middle-class households employed at least one servant. Ours was no exception. My brother and sister and I were raised by our mother, and by Carrie, an African American woman, whom my mother engaged to cook and clean and keep an eye on her children. I loved Carrie very much and would often question, even while very young, this system of servant and master. Why was it that because of my birth into this family of relative privilege, this woman was called upon to serve, and I to be served? As I grew older, I questioned this system more and more, and looked forward to the day when I would learn to serve myself and hopefully others.

When I was in my thirties, my husband and I moved to the country, where we turned our barn into a recording studio. My husband owned a record label, and I found myself feeding and caring for the musicians who came to the recording studio to make albums. Some of these projects were long and drawn out, with the musicians living on and off for months in our home. And, although I had volunteered to play this role, I was often tempted to rebel.

There was one musician, a young woman, singer-songwriter, who was particularly career-centric, and who had the knack of walking into the house from the studio and catching me in compromising domestic predicaments: cleaning toilets, scraping crud out of garbage cans. Though I could appreciate the comedy of the situation, it would remind me of how little progress I was making in my own struggles to find my way as an artist. I was doing plenty of writing at the time but was frustrated by the obstacles to finding a place for my writings. While I was answering the daily needs of those who came to record, so that they might be free to create, my own creative impulses were languishing on the vine (or rather on my computer), and the effort felt doubly difficult. But then, I would reason with myself, why should the world expect these roles to be played by those like Carrie, and not by me? How could I expect to be exempt from this kind of work?

I embraced my role as cook and caretaker only when I viewed it as an act of solidarity with all of those who had cared for me growing up. I willingly served when I was able to see the service as a dedication to those who had served me.

This role of service is one that some born of privilege are never asked to play. More is the pity. A world system where the beds of wealthy children are made by servants is a rickety old thing, and won't stand the ages. Surely children of all walks of life can learn to make their own beds.

Once learned it would be nice to teach them to make up someone's bed whose life is so busily devoted to helping humanity that they absolutely do not have the time to bend over and fluff a pillow. There should be daily sign-up sheets for this sort of service for both children and adults. Who would like to volunteer to make Mahatma Gandhi's bed? Is anyone interested in making dinner for Martin Luther King on Wednesday?

There are plenty of people who need to be served: the poor, the ill, the aged, but not the children of the wealthy. I knew this as a child, and my growing spirit has rebelled against this system ever since.

Jesus came to turn the pyramid scheme upside down.

The pyramid resting on its large end is the symbol of the old kingdom, the one that we live in now, the one that is cracking. The pyramid balanced on its pinnacle represents the new kingdom, with the majority of those on Earth striving to be of use to one another, as we rise to serve.

My very first memory as a child was walking with Carrie down our steep driveway to pick up the mail. I was probably three years old. Carrie held my hand and paused every few feet to let me inspect something on the ground, stare up at trees, stand arrested by a bird's song. If, as I imagine, this was a daily routine, Carrie must have possessed prodigious patience, considering the length of the driveway. The round trip at this pace must have taken about an hour.

When my mother was in the mid-stages of Alzheimer's disease, we would take similar walks together. By this time, I had tasted the sweet fruits of service and had learned its joys. I walked in solidarity with all of those in similar shoes. I am convinced that this number grows every year, that this is the higher plan for us. The old pyramids are crumbling. The humble are rising. Praise God.

17

Just Right

MOST OF us will spend a portion of our early years bemoaning some aspect of our family dynamic. "I was born a sensitive melancholic in a family of enthusiastic optimists," one might say. "Well, I was born a fierce choleric in a family of peaceniks." "I was a gentle apologist in a family of loud barking blowhards." "I was an activist in a family of scaredy-pants." "A clairvoyant in a house of cynics." "Naturally curious in a house full of dullards." I could go on....

My suspicion is that the reaction of one's younger contemporaries might be, "Well, awwww, poor you." Whereas the reaction of a group of people in their later years could be, "Oh, fascinating."

The only statement that might elicit the same response from both young and old could be, "I was born into a perfectly like-minded family where we always agreed on everything."

"Hm… That's a little scary."

I've been thinking lately of what must go on before we decide to come down to planet Earth through the constellation of our families. Some might say, before we return into yet another family dynamic. Whether we've been here before or not, I have to suspect that the family in which we are born is carefully selected to bring out the varied characteristics of our personalities, both treasured and suffered. Let's take a family that has wrestled with addiction for many generations, as fathers, grandmothers, and great uncles fall into the grip of alcoholism. An offspring wrestling with addictions might be tempted to point to family history and lay the blame for his or her inability to embrace sobriety on the shoulders of ancestors. I get that, but the responsibility of healing is the individual's. This disease is spread throughout the world, but it is manifested through the distinct character of the individual. And, though we might say that the disease has come about honestly (through our genetics), the journey and possible recovery will be tailor-made for the person suffering. A son, though he suffers from the same illness as his father, is not his father. A daughter, though she drinks as much as her mother, is not her mother. This is very good news, I feel. The fact that your father was never able to achieve a life of sobriety does not mean that you won't be able to live a sober life.

I suspect, at this point in history, that most family lines will have been tainted by substance abuse or mental illness, or both. My family is not an exception to this rule, with a father who wrestled with bipolar disorder and several uncles who struggled with alcoholism. Both tendencies swim around in the family blood. I heard a man on the radio who had a high-level cabinet position in Washington in one of the previous administrations, a psychiatrist who worked for Health and Human Services, say that if you have a family that claims not to have ever been affected by mental illness or addiction, just wait, tick-tock. He went on to say that, because of his position in Washington in the field of psychiatry, the members of the Congress and Senate had him on speed dial. Many of them either suffered themselves or had family members who were afflicted.

I would like to put forth the argument that these family weaknesses might be as much gifts as they appear to be curses.

Oddly enough, it's our vulnerabilities that most often

lead to our salvation (and by that, I mean awakening), not our strengths. It's in the ground of consequences of difficult behavior that the richest soil exists. This is where we plant the seeds of change. And, if we are careful to water these seeds, we have the opportunity to grow into enlightenment.

I have just finished the book *Release* by a man who wrote under the name Starr Daily. I had read about the book in another book by the psychiatrist George Richie. Dr. Richie would often prescribe *Release* for those of his patients whom he felt were particularly stuck in destructive behavior. It is quite a powerful book, the true story of a hardened criminal's journey from a fierce philosophy of hatred to what he calls the full acceptance of the "law of Love." Daily's religion is love. His life is devoted to love. He wakes at four every morning to spend an hour meditating on love and keeps the flame alight for the rest of the day with thoughts and deeds of love. I found the book life-altering.

Mr. Daily spent twenty years in and out of prison in the early 1900s and his awakening came about as a result of being thrown into solitary confinement and coming very near to death. He had an ecstatic experience with the risen Christ in that dungeon and was never the same. After his encounter, he shared a cell with a character that I would describe as a holy man, a prison lifer, and a patient teacher who guided Mr. Daily through the treacherous beginnings of his new, enlightened life. Daily lived on to lift thousands of souls with his story.

I have a friend whose husband, a doctor, used to work in the field of substance abuse. On some days he attended two interventions a day. Imagine! My friend tells me her husband's coworkers were often recovered alcoholics and drug abusers themselves, and she considered them the most admirable group of people she had ever had the privilege of getting to know. These were therapists and fellow doctors whose lives were devoted to helping people with the same vulnerabilities with which they had struggled. The harrowing journey to the bottom and the climb up and out of misery made for the bravest and kindest of souls. I believe that this brand of heroism is cause for more celebration than much of what we consider meritorious in our world.

Given the possibilities of such soul growth, one might guess that some of the longest lines in the pre-incarnation stage (before we embark on life) are for those families infected with substance abuse and mental illness.

"Oh no," we might impulsively say, "I'm not standing in that line for a cushy, middle class, teetotaling, church-every-Sunday, goody-goody, same-same, level-headed family. No way. Give me a thick crust to crack, give me a challenge, something to tame, something to bust through. I know myself. I won't learn a dang thing in a family of softies."

"Ok," the angels might reluctantly concede. "You asked for it."

Sproing!

"God bless the child."

18

From Here

HAVE I mentioned before that I love stories about near-death experiences? I will read anyone's account of visiting the other side, no matter how awkwardly told, whatever the religious or philosophical bias of the person recounting the tale. I can always tiptoe around the ideology of the teller to look for the little grains of truth. Sometimes these are more like big boulders.

I read a book once by a man who had a near-death experience, which included a movie-like review of his life. It would be an understatement to say that this man had been difficult: a bully as a child and a violent young man, he eventually took a job with the Special Services where he was responsible for the deaths of scores of people.

Once, having received orders to kill a man of some importance in Central America, he grew frustrated by the number of armed guards that surrounded the man and opted to blow up the hotel where this man was staying, killing dozens of innocent people. His life review involved not only the feelings of those who had lost their loved ones, but future generations of children who would not have this person in their lives.

As with all near-death life reviews, there were angelic beings helping this man to have compassion for himself, showing him that his actions were the result of his God-given temperament mixed with his upbringing, and more importantly, helping him to understand that he could at any moment decide to live a very different life, assuring him that underneath his personality was a being of pure love and possibility.

In all of these experiences, the resounding theme is that even when one finds oneself in circumstances that appear very wrong, there is always a way through them and into rightness. One of the reasons that I continue to explore near-death experiences is because I cannot be told enough times to trust in this rightness of life.

This is not an easy concept to convey. I have heard

some people say, "Everything is perfect." Of course it is not. There still exist war, hunger, and slavery, for example, and we cannot rest until life on planet earth is rid of these. The point is, despite all that is decidedly wrong with life, there is always a path toward improvement, toward eventual and eternal good. For the soldier, the starving human, and the slave, there is always hope.

The Stoics of the first century AD repeated this notion again and again. Two of the great champions of the Stoic philosophy were Marcus Aurelius and Epictetus. The first was an emperor and the second a slave. Although they came from widely opposing positions in Roman society, both came to the same conclusion, that life is right.

The message that these two great minds repeatedly attempted to drive home is acceptance. They urge us to accept the role we are given and live secure in the knowledge that it is the very role we were meant to play, and play gracefully.

They do not mean by this that if we are born into slavery we mustn't strive for freedom. They are not urging apathy, resignation, which too often leads to resentment. They are suggesting that the place where you find yourself today is the very place from which it is possible to stride forth into your future. Inherent in the present, there is a way through to fullness, perfect peace, harmony, deep joy—some call this place the Kingdom of Heaven—and you will know it when you reach it. Whether you find it in an imperial palace, or in a slave's cell, you will recognize it.

The psychologist Dan Gottlieb, who hosts an NPR radio show every Monday in my area of the country, has an interesting story. Many years ago he was in a car accident that left him paralyzed from the neck down. At the time he was already a practicing psychologist. Early on, during his recovery in the hospital, he reached a point where he questioned whether he could possibly live the life he was being asked to live in his compromised body. This was a point of reckoning for him. On the same day, one of his nurses asked whether she might come and speak to him after her shift was over when she would have more time. He answered, "Of course," assuming that she wished to offer him comfort.

Later that night the nurse entered his room and sat in a chair next to him.

"Doc," she said, "I've got this problem..." and proceeded to lay out for him the difficulties with which she had been struggling.

Dr. Gottlieb said that it was during this encounter, when he was listening to this woman outline her troubles, that he stopped and faced his future. "Yes," he said to himself, "I can do this." Assured that his lifework would continue, he saw his way through.

I would suggest that the only place from which one can see one's way into a brighter life is from the present moment. It is impossible, if your thoughts are in the past, to see your way into the future. As long as your thoughts are focused on some past hurt, failure, insult, or their opposite, some compliment, success, reward (a rousing success can be more paralyzing to the growth of your spirit than an utter failure), you won't be able to see your forward direction. How can you, when you are standing with your back to it?

A friend of mine suggested that the line from the Lord's Prayer, "Lead us not into temptation" might have more to do with the temptation to let our thoughts lead us into the past rather than any sort of weakness of will in the present.

She knows a man who, after many years, still blames himself for his daughter's suicide. He believes he might have been able to say something, do something, listen differently, to prevent this tragedy from happening. My friend is a parent as well and bleeds for this man.

Lead us not into the temptation of forever punishing ourselves for our past failures, our presumed negligence, or the things we might have taken for granted. Lead us not into the temptation to stand with our backs to the possibilities of our future. In short, turn us around.

There are times, moments in our lives, when we cannot do this ourselves. We must be led. Like a blind person, we must put our hand in another's and be led away from the dark past and up to the hopeful present.

A good friend, a good counselor would never allow us to stand with our backs to the future. They would suggest that we turn around and face what is coming toward us. They might even offer to face it with us and point out the shiny glimmerings of hope.

This place, this present moment, is where we can begin.

I'm thinking of posting a little laminated message on my writing desk.

I'll write it out in big block letters, with a period after every word...

Start. Here. Now.

19

Hesitation

IT'S BEEN well over a year since I noticed the unopened bag of rose food in Rich's yard.

Our neighbor Rich is somewhere in his mid-eighties and has one of the kindest faces I have ever seen: a face that could only be the result of a life's effort of gentleness toward others. Rich can be found most days caring for the rosebushes that surround his house: pruning, feeding, fussing. This is mainly where I have encountered him. I do not know him well, only in passing.

Every morning I pass Rich's house on the way to the park where I walk my dogs and one morning last year, having driven past the house on my way in and out of the park, I dashed back into my house to tell Matt that we needed to go back to the park to hunt for chanterelles. I had spotted the bright orange fungus among the wood's understory. I was home only a half-hour before we headed back out the door on our expedition. Passing Rich's house for the third time that morning, I saw the unopened bag of rose food on the wall. "When is he going to use that?" I wondered as we rounded the corner and I took in the scene in front of the house. There was a body lying next to the wall, eyes closed, cutting shears resting in his hand. It was Rich.

"Stop!" I screeched, as Matt slammed on the brakes. I dove out of the car to run over to where he lay, placing my hand on his arm, his head. He was alive, but just coming back to consciousness.

"Are you ok?" I asked. He mumbled, confused, with his hand covering his head. Matt knocked at the door of the house. We knew that he lived with his invalid wife and two grown daughters. One of the daughters came to the door, sleepy, hair wrapped in a towel.

"Your father's had an accident," Matt tells her. The house wakes up in alarm, an ambulance is called. Both daughters hover, asking their father questions. He seems to have fallen off the wall, blood trickles from one eye. There is a horrible moment when we fear that he might have stabbed himself with his shears. No, we determine, there is no blood on the clippers. His eye, he tells us, hurts terribly. The ambulance comes. The daughters follow. My husband and I drive off. I begin to pray for Rich. Whenever I think of him, I pray for him, and I think of him constantly.

Two days later I am fortunate to find one of the daughters sitting outside the house as I drive home from the park. I hop out of my car and step away from the din of my barking dogs to hear the story of what transpired in the hospital. Apparently, the fall damaged his eye. The pupil was missing altogether. "They might have to remove the eyeball," she tells me. "He is in a great deal of pain." This information twists through my nerves. "Oh, no, no, no, no. Oh, I am so sorry, that sweet man. I am so sorry."

I increase my prayers. A week later I knock on Rich's door with a tin of cookies. He is still in the hospital, his daughters inform me. His eye may not have to be removed after all. They are hopeful, but the sight is gone. "I am so, so sorry," I repeat, and I drive off, praying.

In the coming weeks I grow shy about stopping at the house. I don't want to bother the family. He is not my father, and perhaps they are tired of my questions.

Over the following weeks I grow more and more timid. During this time, I do not see Rich, ever, in his yard. I have always suspected that Rich was as feral as I am, which would make a day spent indoors unthinkable. I couldn't imagine that he would come home and never walk, limp, crawl outside again. Where was he?

Weeks pass, filled with gorgeous weather, but no sign of Rich. Months go by. I rarely see the daughters, and if I do, they are in the back yard with their two small dogs, a sight that whips my two dogs into a frenzy of automobile protection (ear-splitting, window-smudging rampages in the back of my car).

Fall arrives, and then winter, no sign of Rich. One day I see a group of people at the house. A funeral? I check the obituaries. Nothing.

Spring comes and then a lovely, dry summer, perfect for roses and feral people. No Rich. The rose food bag, having been rained on, frozen stiff and thawed out, still rests on the wall. Rich couldn't be alive, I conclude. I stop praying for him and pray that the mourning period for his family will be lightened.

The summer ends and I am in the woods one morning when suddenly the thought of Rich bursts into my mind. "Where are you?" I inwardly ask. "If I knew you were here, I would take up my prayers again. But you couldn't be here. How could you stay indoors during this beautiful season?"

On my way home from the park, I spot one of Rich's daughters walking along the road near my house. I am perfectly positioned to stop and speak with her, but as I come near, I grow shy. "How do I ask whether her father is on this or that side of death?" I wonder. "What words do I use?" My dogs begin to bark. "Oh," I think, "I will just leave her alone." I creep by very slowly, waving and smiling. Suddenly, my youngest dog, Sunshine, goes flying out the back window—how was that window opened?!—She lands on the road, loses her footing, and rolls up to the woman's feet. I stop the car and jump out. Sunshine is fine, just shocked and slightly embarrassed. So are the humans. The ice is broken. "How is your father?" I ask. "Is he still with you in the house?" The right words are there, of course.

"He is still with us," she assures me. "He only has one eye, he has Parkinson's disease and has had a stroke, but he is still at home."

"Oh, I am so glad to know this. I had been wondering. Do you need a ride?" I ask.

"No," she declines, smiling, "I'm walking to the little church around the corner."

We exchange a few more words and I pull into my driveway.

Two hours later when I leave my driveway again,

miracle of miracles, I spot Rich's other daughter pushing a man in a wheelchair. There is no question of not stopping.

"Oh, I am so glad to see you, Rich. And, out on this beautiful day."

Rich's health has had little effect on his face. If anything, his countenance has grown even gentler. "A face blessed by brotherly love," I think.

We visit for a moment and I drive off, grateful. I roll down the road, making all sorts of promises to the heavens. "I won't ever let shyness keep me from stopping to speak, or check an impulse to enquire after a neighbor," I promise.

And, if I am tempted to go back on my vow I have only to look at the slight pink scar on Sunshine's chin from that day. "Oh, bless you, sweetheart, "I tell her, "You took one for the team."

20

Drunk Again

RECENTLY I made a request to the heavens to help me with an old habit. I was growing tired of my inner critic, in fact so tired that I wanted to kick the guy out for good. I have wasted far too much precious thought analyzing and coming up with prescriptions for what ails people's psyches. I had been working on trying to detach from disapproving thoughts for many years, yet would still occasionally catch myself looping around ways in which people could improve themselves. On the day that I made my request, I was inwardly schooling a neighbor (whom I barely knew) on the benefits of truthful dialogue with her difficult spouse. I thought I knew exactly how this conversation should go.

I very rarely speak these thoughts to the people about whom I am thinking them, having concluded that they are none of my business. Therefore, I am essentially the only one who has to listen to me. It's just me, and little old me, and I was fed up with me.

One morning, on my daily contemplative walk, I asked for some substantial help with this issue. I wanted to wipe out the inner nosey-pants for good.

I understand that we are all wrestling with the temperaments with which we were born, and these are affected by our upbringing, our philosophies, religions, the culture in which we live. None of us is without some level of dysfunction. I have argued with myself, tried to wrestle with my critic, thrown the wisdom of the ages at her.

"How can you say, 'Brother, let me take out the speck that is in your eye,' when you yourself do not see the log that is in your own?" Jesus is making an excellent argument here, but I am a hard sell.

I've tried using the little Buddhist story of the traveling teacher and his student. I'll share it with you now.

Two Buddhists are walking along a road, one is a teacher and the other his student. After some time, they approach a stream that they must wade through in order to continue. As they come to the crossing another student runs up to the teacher.

"Teacher, will you carry me across the stream? I don't want to get my feet wet."

The teacher, without hesitation, picks the young man up, carries him across the water, and deposits him on the other side of the stream. The young man skips off with lovely dry feet, while the teacher and his student squish on in damp-sandal silence. After about a mile the student explodes with exasperation, turning to his teacher, "That was outrageous of that guy to ask you to carry him across the water! He was disrespectful, self-serving, and didn't even thank you."

"Yes," replies the teacher, "all of that is true, but I put him down a mile ago and you are still carrying him."

I find it interesting that just when I think my well-polished philosophy has allowed me to transcend something such as criticism of my fellow man, just then a criticism so huge, so philosophy-flattening will come along that I will be thrown to my knees. I'd been looping around my neighbor's issues for days

"Damn," I think, "drunk again!"

"Please, please, please take this critical voice away from me," I begged the heavens, "I am mad-weary of its nonsense."

I am not sure of the exact timing when I suffered my painful reckoning. It could have arrived as quickly as the next day, but I certainly didn't see it coming.

One afternoon, in a matter of half an hour, I went from a completely healthy, reasonable human being to a desperately agitated maniac. I was suffering a sudden onset of a raging bladder infection.

The attack was acute and vicious and the pain medicine, which typically takes an hour to give relief, wasn't touching the torment. I writhed around the house in a mixture of unbearable pain and mad-raw nerves. Imagine the worse toothache you've ever had and multiply it by fifteen. I took another pill.

At some point around hour three, I lay down on my bed and tried to calm myself. I didn't manage to reach a state that resembled anything like peace but, after a while, I began to think about all of the people in the world without access to healthcare. Although my medicine was taking an excruciatingly long time to take effect, and I was wondering whether I had misdiagnosed the episode and should be headed to the hospital, at least I knew that there was a hospital within reach. I have traveled to many places in the world where this is not the case.

In rural Haiti, a woman in my predicament would

have to walk for days to reach a place where she might find relief and then wait for hours to be seen by someone.

I tried to imagine it and the idea was unthinkable. I thought of how privileged I was and how profoundly sad it was that anyone would go through pain such as I was experiencing without hope of relief. I went further with this thought, deeper. I thought of how difficult the human condition is and how fragile we are in our earthly bodies, bodies that can turn into little torture chambers in an instant. I went further, deeper. I thought of how fragile our emotional systems are, our psyches, when in a moment we could be thrown into shocking, agonizing grief by the loss of a child, a spouse.

I finally reached a place where I was so utterly sorry for everyone, no exception, everyone who occupied or had ever occupied a human body. I was just so very sad for them. Slowly, very slowly my pain began to subside. The pain medication was taking effect. After four hours of misery, I could breathe normally, rest easily, begin to release my tense nerves.

I knew that I had been somewhere profound. I was beginning to heal, a true healing, which always involves some drip of enlightenment.

I thought of my neighbor whom I presumed didn't know how to speak to her difficult husband. Who was I to give counsel in a world where there existed the potential of such sudden and acute suffering? I do not know this woman's fears or sufferings. I have never spent one moment inside of her psyche.

And more to the point, if I knew that the one I was inwardly criticizing was at that moment suffering an earthquake of anguish, would I proceed with my thinking? Of course not. If I knew that the person I was criticizing was suffering crushing torment, how would I treat them with my thoughts? I would treat them with prayer, and nothing more.

Enough said.

21

Step, Stop,
Turn Back, Lift

I ATTENDED SIX schools during my years of education and although there were elements of competition in all of them, two stood out as being particularly miserable with the stuff. One school I attended from the ages of twelve to fifteen and the other from nineteen to twenty-one. The first inspired the student body to hustle for the best grades, and the second, a performing arts school, for the most coveted roles in the school's theatrical productions. I experienced both as icy, bloodless battlegrounds and suffered wholeheartedly during my attendance there.

The spirit of competition continued to haunt my psyche for much of the first half of my life as I attempted to find work as an actor and then as a playwright. Although I could no longer identify my competition, as I could my fellow classmates at school, I was distressed by the nameless individuals who were pulling ahead of me in the race to find meaningful work. Considered realistically, I was working against the odds: 90% unemployment in the actor's union and easily the same percentage of plays rejected every year.

I have heard that in the old Hollywood days, when the big studios had contracts with their lead actors, that the three top dogs (male or female) who got the juiciest parts, would feel that they were in competition with one another, sometimes to the point of obsession. Even though there were millions of people in the country who would have loved to be in their shoes, the only shoes they could think of were the ones worn by their competition.

We are trained at an early age to compete, to race each other, beat each other at some game. We love hearing that we are the best, love winning awards, love being at the top of our field. The system is engrained in our culture. It is what drives many toward achievement. Some do achieve grand things, but at such a price: friendships lost, bodies broken, ethics tossed. If there were no one in our chosen field of endeavor, no one against whom to pit our efforts, would we work as hard to attain our goals? I believe that if we truly loved the effort, we would do much better than attain our goals, we would love our lives.

If it were possible to wave a wand and destroy the illusion of competition and cause everyone to give it up altogether, all of the people on the earth at the same time, I know that I would be one of those joyfully waving away.

I strongly suspect that if we could view ourselves through the eyes of God, we would see that no one is any greater than another, see that we are all the same size, that being bigger and better than another is an impossibility. Take away all the constraints of the finite world, take away time, body, personality, place, and relative privilege of birth, take away everything but the soul and its connection to God, and we would see that the idea of competing against one another is nonsensical, like stepping on our own heads to appear larger.

When I lived in New York I used to chuckle at the lines of the song *New York, New York:*

"I want to wake up in a city that doesn't sleep.
And find I'm king of the hill, top of the heap."

*   *   *

"Oh dear," I thought to myself, "how unfriendly."

In C. S. Lewis's book *That Hideous Strength*, the narrative follows a man who strives, in a sense, to be king of the hill. This character enters a corporation with a substantial hierarchy and is eager to rise in the company. It is a fascinating study of the human desire to achieve greater and greater security, status, recognition. Lewis describes this corporate ascension as moving from one circle to another (imagine a wedding cake), with the driving desire to attain admission in the innermost, upper circle. This circle of circles is the place where presumably there would be no more striving, no more fear of failure, and where all competition would be unnecessary.

In order to rise, or in this case, achieve a place nearer to the inner circle, Lewis's protagonist is expected to do one slightly unscrupulous thing, perform a mildly unethical act. He does so, with one eye shut to his conscience, only to find that the next circle is not a circle at all, but a group of competing coworkers. He still isn't safe, still isn't secure, and so he strives to gain access to the next circle which requires something a little more unsavory. He is willing, having grown used to the loss to his integrity from the previous transgression, only to find out that this circle holds no more security than the last, with each man for himself in dogged competition. He continues on his journey to reach the central circle, committing acts that are more and more unprincipled, until he reaches the center. I hope you will pick up the book to read Lewis's description of what he discovers there. Suffice it to say that the man finds this inner circle to be an utter sham and realizes that the drive behind his struggle to reach it was based wholly on lies.

One argument against communism and in favor of capitalism is that people don't achieve at a high level if they are not competing. I don't believe this for a moment. I suspect just the opposite is true: competition hinders us, distracts us from achieving great things because we are so focused on the other guy that we lose sight of what we are doing. I don't believe that either political system has a leg up on the other in achievement. My sense is that achievement, real achievement of things that truly matter to mankind, is born of love. Love of the work, love of mankind, love of truth, beauty, and justice. Martin Luther King achieved much, even though he was taken from life before he saw the results of that achievement, and even though the results are not yet fully realized. He was able to achieve what he did because he loved the people he was working for.

In the recent summer Olympics, a young female runner witnessed a fellow runner fall and stopped to help her. This story was very big news. Amazing, that a competitive athlete would choose to help another at the expense of her own success. Wouldn't it be lovely to live in a culture where this was expected, where this was the norm?

Yet haven't we been schooled by all of the great teachers of humanity to stop and help our fellow man? "Until all sentient beings are free," the Bodhisattva vow proclaims, the enlightened will not rest. The idea is echoed by the Christian parable of the shepherd who will not move forward with his flock until he has gone back to help the one lost sheep.

Some bright day we will all understand that the progress of the human race is a united effort and any system based on leaving the fallen in the dust in our efforts to get ahead will only lead to suffering.

No, no.

The progress of humanity goes like this: step, stop, turn back, lift.

And again...

22

Our Big Beautiful Selves

I HAVE A friend who is a writer, a wordsmith, who has begun to have difficulties locating his words. The clinical term for this is aphasia. The condition began by swallowing up one word here or there and is now capable of gulping whole sentences. Understanding him can be a stimulating exercise in deduction and intuition. And, though at times I can sense my friend's frustration, and can see why many might view this problem as a sad, ironic calamity, I must tell you that at some point in every conversation with him, the two of us will end up in a snorting laugh fest.

I wonder whether other people, when talking with someone whose brains are not functioning as they used to, will attempt to provide the missing vocabulary and go utterly blank themselves, as if the malfunction were contagious. "You know the guy who works for that man…" "Yes, I do know exactly who you are talking about," I might say, "but I'll be damned if I can come up with his name at this moment." If a wrong name is interjected, all bets are off. "Is it Marvin?" "No! oh no! all chance of recall has just been smashed to smithereens!" This name game is sure to happen during every conversation with my friend. At some point we will find ourselves staring off into the distance waiting for the vagabond name to crest the arid hills of our minds.

My friend still closely follows our country's political news and still manages to get across his opinions and his good store of historical, political knowledge. Though he is able to voice the occasional complete sentence, he more often falls into linguistic potholes. When this happens, he will fill the holes with hints and facial expressions. Occasionally a thought will be reduced to just a couple of words. While trying to speak of the policies of a local political candidate the other day, and wishing to convey that this woman was in favor of stricter gun laws, he had only to say, "bang, bang," and all was clear.

I understand why we lament the loss of a man's abilities, a woman's strengths, especially those most dominant. I can see why some would say, "but it's so unfair to take away from a man the one thing that has been his life's blood, or the gift that has been her livelihood." Perhaps, but I would like to suggest that when these things drop away, we're sometimes allowed the opportunity to discover who the person was beyond the gift. We're offered a glimpse of the greater spirit behind this one earthly personality. The loss that appears so wrong to us may have some rightness in it.

It's possible to become dependent on a talent, like a crutch, and believe that you cannot exist without it. This can happen to anyone: an artist, athlete, entrepreneur, scientist. If the talent has caused you to become atrophied in other areas of your life, then the gift has succeeded in making you smaller, more restricted as a human. It has formed a tight shell around you. It may be best to let it crack and peel away.

My husband Matt played pick-up basketball for years, well into his fifties, until his knees began to bother him. He dreaded the day when he would have to face life without this outlet, believing it to be the secret to his sanity. Eventually his doctor told him that he either had to quit playing or suffer much greater consequences as he aged. He took up hiking. Hiking in turn has given him some of his most treasured memories in the years since this decision: hours and hours of walking in the quiet woods, discoveries of little-known trails around our county, and finally major hikes to Machu Picchu, Peru and El Mirador, Guatemala. His world opened up as a result of his willingness to put aside something that no longer served him. Dashing back and forth on a basketball court could never compare to hiking the Andes.

I have spent many years hosting musicians in my home who have come to work with my husband. The younger ones tend to be caught up in their professions and rarely talk of anything else (though there are exceptions), whereas the older ones are able to talk about everything under the sun. When I meet an older musician whose conversation does not move beyond the confines of the music business, I am tempted to tiptoe up to bed. It's like listening to a mother who is unable to talk of anything but her fifty-year-old child.

The other day after a difficult hour or so of writing I grew frustrated. I'd gone sour on myself and needed some distance from my cluttered head. I took a walk, visited a couple of horses, and chatted with some friends, after which I felt much better. Later that day while talking with my husband, I said. "I'm not a writer, I'm a person who happens to write." The truth of this might seem obvious, but there are many who get caught up in defining themselves by what they do, and their moods will swing around every success and frustration they encounter. Best to be a human first.

Here's a question. Would you rather be introduced to someone at a party as a member of your profession? "This is the lawyer I was telling you about." Your aptitude? "This is the artist I mentioned to you." Your achievements? "This is the CEO I spoke of." Or would you prefer the intro to be your relation to the one introducing you? Here is my favorite: "This is my good friend Margaret." I puff up like a pigeon, get all fluffy-hearted. When you are introduced as a friend, you have already been invited into the other's heart, no awkward social barriers to deal with. On the other side of this equation, if one is meeting for the first time someone very famous for his or her achievements, say a Nobel Peace Prize winner, wouldn't it be lovely to be introduced to them without the grand title? Wouldn't it be more comfortable to meet them as a possible new friend? "This is my good friend Desmond." "Hi Desmond, I'm Margaret." Better to be a friend than an award. Friends don't gather dust.

I've been compiling a mental list of words and people's names that have gone missing from the neighborhood of my mind. When challenged, I might say, "Oh no, that name's gone on a walkabout, we may not see him for months." There are some words, as far as I can tell, that might have fallen off of the edge of the planet by now. This might be an argument to cultivate younger, sharper friends with vast vocabularies, but I don't know about that. We're so much more than words. I'm more interested these days in the big, beautiful soul underneath all of those trappings. Trappings, that's a pretty good word. "Who are you behind all of those trappings? Those things that have trapped you into thinking you cannot be summed up without them?"

Given the possible benefits, it might be best to look at the loss of any ability, whether to play an instrument, to write an essay, to run a marathon, to run a country, as an opportunity to discover our greater selves. "Oh, thank you, fates," we might say, "thank you. I was feeling awfully small and confined by all of that talent. Whew."

23

The Pasture

ONE TYPE of news reporting that has me plugging my ears and humming these days is that in which a news team travels into a town to sniff out the most ignorant citizen in the community and places a microphone in front of him. As if to say, "look at this guy, tell me he isn't the thickest member of the herd." My first reaction is, "Oh my, you mean there are people in this country who actually think that way?" And then I might sum them up. "That's got to be the biggest beef-head in the pasture." So unfriendly! I don't like those thoughts! So, when I think a story is headed for one of these pastures, I go running for the hills. I don't need any excuse to love people less. I need reasons to love them more.

* * *

My brother reminded me the other day of Howard Storm, a man who had a remarkable near-death experience in the mid-nineties, a story that he outlined in his book, *My Descent into Death*. Howard claims to have had a remarkable encounter with Jesus, an experience that entirely changed his life. During this encounter, as is the case with so many near-death experiencers, he was told that he must return to his life. And it was further suggested that Howard had important work to do for God on Earth. Until this encounter, Howard was a fierce atheist and could not imagine how he would be able to do any sort of important work for God.

Jesus told him that he was simply to love the person that he was with, whoever that person was, and that would change the world.

"But that is too simple," Howard replied, "and it will never work."

"It will work, Jesus answered. "One person will love another, and that person will carry that love, and love another, until the world is filled with love. The world will be changed by love from one to another."

Howard continued to argue with Jesus, explaining how the plan had all sorts of holes in it.

"Do you think you are the only one in God's plan?" Jesus replied, "There are millions of people changing the world and millions more becoming part of the plan."

Of course, of course, the plan would be this simple, simple and difficult at the same time, putting all of the responsibility on the individual.

My friend Sarah has a fantasy that the entire family of man will one day experience a reset moment. One day, she likes to imagine, there will be a voice from the sky, which everyone in the world will hear, and we will all, every single one of us, look up and listen. Whatever the voice says to us, it will usher in a time of peace and healing around the whole globe, and a saving of our dear planet.

I once had a dream where I heard the voice of God. I have written of this somewhere else, but I think I have come to a deeper understanding of its meaning.

I was walking up a great hill, and next to me walked a man whom I understood viewed me as being slightly beneath him. He was Muslim, and I could tell that he assumed that I was a Christian. We lived in a town where Christians were in the minority. I was also a woman, a fact for which I believed he also judged me as being beneath him. And, though we walked fairly near to one another, and at the same pace, I felt him purposefully looking ahead at the road, careful not to glance in my direction.

I viewed his attitude toward me as a failing in him and thought it slightly comical that he could not bring himself even to look over and acknowledge my presence. We walked like this for some time when suddenly, out of the sky, boomed the voice of God. I stopped.

"Did you hear that?" I asked the man.

"Yeah, I heard it." He answered, without looking at me, and began to walk on.

I scampered up after him, saying to his back, "That was the voice of God."

He hesitated. "Yeah," he grunted, still unwilling to turn his head in my direction.

"But, did you hear what he said?" I asked him.

He mumbled that maybe he hadn't quite caught it.

I moved to face him. "He said, 'Bless your sweet reunion."

The man turned to me and our eyes met. At which point, any prejudice either of us held toward the other vanished.

* * *

One universal, shared by those who have had near-death experiences and those who have had ecstatic epiphanies, is the awareness of the perfect union of all of life, from molecules to stars. This is an idea that is echoed among the mystics and the teachings of the great spiritual masters. For those who have managed to attain this understanding, words can be too small to convey its magnitude. And, however difficult this idea is to speak of, it is much more difficult to live it out.

If we are to believe our spiritual teachers, and trust those who have arrived at the truth of the unity of all of life, then our journey through life should be a process of striving for this sense of unity with all of mankind, and finally with all creation.

But, here is my question: Why?... Why is it necessary that we leave the heavens, where we knew this unity, to come down here to live out a lifetime in a place of widely accepted disparity? Why? Why is it that we are asked to live out a life of apparent duality, with me and you, them and us, black and white, Muslim and Christian, male and female, sane and insane? Why? Why do we travel to this place of apparent disunity and then struggle to uncover its coherence? There must be some use in this process for our individual souls.

Perhaps we can only learn certain lessons about love

while living out a life in apparent isolation. Love is certainly more challenging when we think of ourselves as separate from those around us. Maybe if we can learn to love from a place of supposed division, we will have attained super-powers of love.

To return to the cow pasture, I don't believe we came here to gain enough independence to be able to point out the weakest link in the herd. "Would you look at that crazy bovine?" No. I suspect it has more to do with looking for what, in our shared pasture, we can love together, what unites us. We can love the same sweet grass, the same bright flowers, the same clear sky, the same pure water, the same fresh air, the ground of our shared mother earth.

"God bless the herd," we will shout out, "God bless the pasture." We will sing, "God bless our sweet reunion."

24 ❀

Good Cheer

MY FRIEND Hayden suggests that as we age and grow less cute, we might be wise to compensate for the loss of good looks with good cheer.

Emerson writes, "There is no beautifier of complexion, or form, or behavior like the wish to scatter joy and not pain around us."

My friend Patty, who has made it into her sixties with a congenital kidney disease, likes to tell her body every day how proud she is of it. How grateful she is that it has bravely fought to give her a long life on the planet.

I am beginning to suspect that for those of us who have been graced with long life, the attainment of self-love could be our last challenge to enlightenment. I am not talking about ego, or pride, but a certain grateful recognition for the bodies that have carried us through our years on the earth and will hopefully carry us far into old age. Our earthly clothing, or temporary housing, might be viewed as a sort of mobile home. These vehicles undoubtedly benefit from our care and attention to maintenance but eventually they will break down. They were not built to last forever. To criticize them when they begin to show the inevitable signs of age seems rather small-spirited of us. "Oh, look at that rust spot on the passenger door, unsightly!" we might say. "My roof looks like hell, my tires are all bald, there are pebble cracks in every window, my wiper blades fell apart years ago, and there are no replacements for this model. This old beater is a piece of junk."

The poor thing!

Wouldn't it be kinder to say, "Oh, this grand old tank of mine has carried me through so much: through days of blistering heat, nights of frigidity, through wild storms, and traffic jams so backed up we thought we'd never move again. What a blessing this dear old jalopy has been."

Patty's husband Chris gave her one of his kidneys several years ago. I'd say he's pretty well set for an eternity of Christmas gifts. This organ, twice the size of either of Patty's original kidneys, works like a bear. This isn't the only calamity Patty's mobile home has suffered. She's has had breast cancer, twice. She's pitched out of and over just about everything. She's had car accidents, horse accidents, dog accidents—that's when you trip over a dog and break your bones—her body has been carved up, patched together and rearranged, but she's still rolling. And she is rolling with enormous good cheer.

Patty likes to say to her body, "I love you, you are enough. You are enough for me." After which she might take the dear old thing out for some fresh air and fruit.

Some, when faced with living out a life in a compromised body, will suggest, "Well, consider the alternative," by which, of course, they mean death. But death, the transition out of our meat-suits (as my friend Christine calls her body), and into our heavenly suits, is not only inevitable but, I presume, a welcome change, like going on a long camping trip and finally returning home to take a hot bath and put on fresh clothes. Delicious!

My friend Sarah refers to any uncomplimentary, old age rumination as "Methuselah thinking." This is when one sees oneself as an ancient ruin, of no more use to society than an old phone booth. Remarkably, Sarah will be haunted by this thinking, even though she is a teacher in New York City school system, with a little army of adoring child followers. If the criticism that we sometimes visit on our aging selves came from someone else, we would consider it heartless. "Look at that thing? It can hardly climb a hill these days without sputtering. And that paint job! Pathetic!"

Sarah tells me that she will perform certain tasks, such as thoroughly cleaning her kitchen after her evening meal, as an exercise in self-love. "Let's do this for Sarah," she says to herself, "She will be so happy in the morning to wake to a sparkling kitchen as she dashes to get ready for the day."

I'm considering adopting this practice. "Oh dear, Margaret seems to be having an ancient day, today," I might say to myself, "Maybe she needs a lift? Let's take her out for a spin, give her a little shot of sunshine."

Self-love is a tricky assignment, made more interesting as our bodies age.

It appears that the most dreadful thing that could be said of the aging is, "Oh, she's let herself go, poor thing. Such a shame." Or, "Look at that guy, he's a shadow of his former self." I was just on vacation with an eighty-three-year-old friend who asked where she might find a scale to weigh herself every day. She didn't want to put on a pound. Good gravy! When do we get to let go of that crazy gym teacher in our heads?!

There was a couple in my hometown that prided themselves on their resolve not to gain a pound more than they weighed on their wedding day. They made a pact and managed to keep it to the day they died. They considered it one of their greatest accomplishments. Sigh.

This tight grip on our youth can be so limiting. Every age offers us its gifts. Perhaps we should be flattered when someone suggests we have "let ourselves go." "Hooray," we might counter, "I've been working toward that goal my entire life."

"Youth is wasted on the young," they say, but perhaps we could say the same of aging. "Age is wasted on the aging." It is certainly wasted when we grumble about our mobile homes, when we refuse to let go of the way we rolled in our younger years, when we fuss about our paint job, our tire pressure, our power steering...

Patty, in order to thank her body for its resilience, will take it out to a yoga class. "Let me do you a favor," she will offer, "let me take you out to a stretch class, make you feel better."

I suspect the best fuel on which we could run our

mobile homes is simple appreciation. No matter the make or model, the finest, most energy-efficient food for our bodies is probably gratitude.

I'm thinking of a new daily practice. "Good morning, you dear old thing," I might say to my body. "What a fine job you've been doing all these years. Don't let anybody tell you otherwise, and especially don't take any grief from that person who lives in your head. You are enough, dear, you are enough." After this reassuring pep talk, I might offer it something, an outing of some sort.

"Today, my good friend, I'm going to fill your tank with love, and roll around the neighborhood, waving a cheerful hand." I might offer. "Let's go, shall we? We'll toot around with the windows open, blowing kisses to the world."

25

The Keys to Confidence

I HAVE NEVER learned the secret to perfect confidence. Though there are many skills that I employ on a daily basis—writing, cooking, to use a couple of examples—I am unwilling to refer to myself as a writer or a cook. Both endeavors are entered into with a healthy dose of baked-in self-doubt. I always pray before I pick up the pen or the spatula.

This natural timidity has never allowed me to claim any sort of expert status and hence I have avoided the presumption of teaching another how to do anything. However, there is one exception. There is one skill that I possess, and have possessed for many years, that does not come with any attendant doubts, a skill that I put into practice often, whenever I can, and will teach others without apology, even with bravado. I speak of the art of parallel parking.

Many years ago, when I was in my late twenties, I lived on the Isle of Manhattan, a land so conscientious about keeping its streets sparkly that its inhabitants are expected to move their cars from one side of the street to the other every other day for street cleaning. As a good citizen of this fair city and excellently skilled, I felt, in the art of parallel parking, I willingly performed my duty. Every other day I would dash out the door of my apartment building, hop behind the wheel and execute the no-nonsense moves of my perfect practice. Until one day...

My husband had recently purchased a large, awkward van and I had volunteered to move the vehicle that day. I was a tad late in leaving my apartment and so discovered only one smallish space left into which to squeeze my bulging vehicle. "No problem," I thought to myself, "I'm a master. I'll have this tucked in like a slice of bread in no time." I hopped in, threw it into drive, then reverse, bold turn, reverse, bold turn, drive, scronk! Something went desperately wrong. I leapt out the door, ran to the back end of the van, and froze with horror. My back fender was curled around the front fender of the car behind in a perfect handshake, metal embracing metal. It was obvious that none of my fancy moves from this point would extricate one bumper from the other. There was no algebraic solution to the dilemma. I stood stunned and appalled.

Pedestrians walked by and commented. "Whoa, good luck with that one!" they chuckled, "How did you manage that?! You're gonna rip that guy's fender right off!" More people gathered, each reporting on their findings, "Whew, that is one mess you have going on there!" No one gave helpful advice, theirs was all snarky journalism. They sneered and snorted and stated the obvious. I considered crying to make them stop, but could only muster a groan. Time slowed to a crawl, allowing me to look into the past and rue the day that I had ever presumed to imagine myself an expert, and allowing me to peer into the future on the streets of my fair city, contending with nosey pedestrians, tow trucks and irate car owners.

I moaned some more as comments continued to be hurled from the sidewalk when I heard a voice next to me. "I think I can get you out of that." Turning to its source, still speechless, I wondered whether it was the voice of God.

The voice, which was tinged with a hint of an accent, emanated from a slight, olive-skinned man of about thirty-five years. If I had to guess, I would say he was of Middle Eastern descent. But more notable was his attitude of thoughtful confidence. This was something I had never managed myself, but which I could recognize in another. Without uttering a word I held out my keys to him.

The next five minutes were sprinkled with fairy dust. I cannot fathom how he managed to perform the task without ripping the bumpers off both cars, but manage he did, without causing the slightest touch of metal on metal. My audience of bystanders and I watched in awe as he made his gentle movements. This was a true master, able to perform the miraculous with so little effort that I wondered if he had cast a spell on us. When he stepped out of the van I found my voice. "God bless you!"

He smiled and walked away, his audience watching in stunned silence. Though it has been close to thirty-five years since this incident occurred, I continue to think of this man and when I do I ask for a blessing on him.

I have two friends who make beautiful food. One is a woman and one a man. When my female friend makes a meal, she will deliver it to the table with numerous apologies. "I think I cooked it too long this time. It was better the last time I made it. I think it could be a bit spicier, don't you? It calls for a hint of sugar but I think it could use a bit more."

My male friend, on the other hand, delivers the food to the table with gusto. "You gotta taste this! It's the best thing you'll ever put in your mouth!" He studies you as you take the first bite, "Huh? See what I'm talking about? Amazing, right?!"

I was telling a friend about these two approaches to serving food and asked if she thought that this was a universal difference between the way a woman and a man deliver food to the table. "Actually," my friend replied, "I would say that the same psychology drives both behaviors. Both are acting out of insecurity." I found this to be a highly useful observation.

I must admit to leaning toward the apologetic and have to watch myself so that I don't depress the enthusiasm of my dinner guests before they touch their food. When one apologizes too fiercely for what one has created, there is the danger that the taste of the person who is set to swallow it will be biased to reject it. This goes for any creation from a meal to a piece of writing. When I began to write plays in my early thirties, I would send my creations around to prospective theaters with such a list of apologies that they were bound to overlook the piece. "This is my first play, and I am well aware that it needs a ton of work. Feel free to be as tough with your criticism as you feel necessary. In fact, why don't you just throw it directly into the trash." I hope I have learned a few things over the years. Now I am more apt to say, "Let me make you a meal," or "here is a play I wrote." That seems enough. Oh, and then there is love, hopefully, I offer both with love.

The man who extricated my van's bumper all those years ago was performing an act of loving-kindness. He loved his fellow man enough to offer a kindness to a stranger. He was skilled, no doubt, but there was something more.

These days, when I offer to teach a friend's kid how to parallel park, I do so with a proper dose of humility. "I will show you what I know," I say to them, "but I am not a master. There have been times when all talent fails... I met a master once," I will continue, "a true master. He had that pure confidence, the rare sort, the stuff that stems from love... Beautiful."

26 ❀

When to Take Your Temperature

WHEN I was in college, I rented a house near campus, which I proceeded to fill with roommates. At some point, one of the inhabitants started seeing a young woman who would occasionally stay over at the house. I liked her and thought she was a nice addition to our group. The next month when the rent came due someone brought up whether or not we should charge this girl a bit of rent. I didn't think it would be right and I thought I should make this clear to her. "I don't think it's right to charge you for rent when you are being charged by the college for a dorm room. So please don't worry about it." Within the week, I heard from a friend that she had overheard this young woman telling someone that I had wanted to charge her rent for the nights that she spent in our house. I was horrified. How had I managed to be so misunderstood? In fact, I could be accused of few qualities more abhorrent to me than that of being ungenerous.

Very near this time another friend said to me, "You're not as bad as they say you are, are you, Margaret?" "And who might 'they' be?" I inquired. "Well..." he responded, a bit embarrassed, and went on to tell me who the person was who was spreading these rumors and it was then that I understood. The gossip originated with a young man whose romantic attentions I had not reciprocated, and he was put out. But how was I to save my reputation? I'm not sure I ever did. The truth is, once the poison of false criticism has been leaked, like an oil spill, it is very difficult to clean up. I was to leave that school soon after, and I daresay there are those among the alumni who still believe me to be a tight-fisted, manipulative miser. Sigh.

A year later, after I had moved to New York City, I was to run into this young woman, and again say something to her that was entirely misread. Again I felt terrible that she had misunderstood me, and again I had to let the misunderstanding go, as I knew it was even more impossible to salvage my reputation from the rubble it had become in her mind.

The fact is, no amount of public relations effort on my part would have repaired the damage. Once one has swallowed the poison of a lie, the only hope of relationship repair is for those whose minds have been tainted to move in closer and learn the truth. Or, and this will also work, to discover that the person spreading the falsehood is not to be trusted. Consider the source, they say.

I have been reminded of this history, recently, because a similar situation has arisen, with a woman whom I barely know unjustly accusing me of being both tightfisted and—even worse in my estimation—stingy-hearted to someone whom my husband and I had hired many years ago, and whose job for us was coming to an end.

My first reaction, having listened to this woman's harangue in shocked silence, was to repeat to myself, "God knows who I am. I mustn't be too upset. God knows precisely who I am."

My second response was less high-minded and involved days of mental rebuttal. Like a defense attorney on a deadline, my mind was madly grasping at arguments to clear my reputation. I studied the files of our compensation to this employee and found it to be quite fair. I then went to my computer and began to construct a letter parrying each of the untruths leveled against me by this employee's fierce champion. This missive was coming together nicely, the truths lining up in perfect opposition to the falsehoods, when at some point I came to my senses and managed to raise my head above my indignation. I had to admit that no matter what I did, the poison that had been introduced would probably not so easily be washed away. I also understood that if I allowed the feelings of outrage to have their way with me, my soul would become as sullied as the atmosphere around this rumor.

My conclusion was that it was best to step away and detach from the situation. As with the incident in college, I discovered that the rumors were initiated by insecurity. Our employee was undoubtedly feeling insecure about her future and was grumbling against our treatment of her. Matt and I had been discussing a compensation package for this woman to ease her fears and were in the middle of our talks when her friend and champion went on the attack. This was potentially a disastrous time to attack us for a lack of generosity, making it even more important that I divorce myself of any ill will that might be left over from the accusation of stingy-heartedness. We needed to be cleanly open-handed.

In speaking about this with a friend, she said, "Then it seems to me, you will be rewarding your employee's bad behavior. How does that help?" I wasn't sure how to answer her but felt very strongly that my intuition was correct.

I suspect when we find ourselves looping and looping around a past offense and mentally lining up arguments of defense, it's time to stop and take our temperature. How hot are we? Outrage is corrosive, not only destructive for those whose feelings are piqued but also to those around them. It's a virus that we may not wish to pass on to our loved ones. Quarantine is the best course, I believe, until the fever has passed.

Being unfairly attacked has the power to knock us off our feet, scramble our inner moral compass, and cause us to respond in puny-hearted ways. To turn the other cheek is not only wise advice for stopping the escalation of conflict, but it also puts to death the effects of insult before they have taken root. The truth is, indignation will eat away at the soul with much more devastating consequences than the original offense. It can cause mistrust and cynicism.

George MacDonald on the subject of being unfairly judged writes, "Let a man do right, nor trouble himself about worthless opinion; the less he heeds tongues, the less difficult will he find it to love men." And, this is the real issue, isn't it, this return to the work of loving our neighbors?

I would suggest taking any past indignation and writing it on a piece of paper. Now, fold it into the shape of an airplane, draw back the arm, and let the thing fly. Perfect.

Now, back to the work of life.

27 ❀

Stage Serenity

WHEN I was a young actress I never stepped onto a stage without bone-rattling stage fright. Where is it that I read that the majority of people are more afraid of public speaking than they are of death?

In order to fool myself into appearing in front of an audience, I would attempt to convince myself that there was no one out beyond the stage lights. This never worked, of course, so instead I would try to envision a wall along the proscenium between me and those in the theater seats. This concept of the fourth wall helps you and your fellow actors imagine that you are alone, living out the life of a scene with one another. But I was not using the idea of the fourth wall to aid me to be more authentic, I was employing it to keep myself from jumping out of my skin with terror.

After many years of avoiding any sort of public performance, perhaps fifteen years after I had stepped off the stage for the last time, I found myself once more in the lion's den, facing my worst fears. I had decided to organize a political fundraiser. And, because I was feeling rather passionate about politics, I wished to speak at the event. It was 2006 and the Iraq war had been going on for some time. There was a veteran of that war running for the U.S. Congress in my district. His thoughts on the lies that led to our involvement and his desire to bring the troops home aligned with my own. I wanted to write an introductory speech for this candidate and deliver it to my community. The trouble was, I had not come an inch nearer to uncovering the key to stage serenity.

I launched a prayer campaign. At the same time, I wrote the speech, easily lining up all of my points on paper, and stepped out onto the long road of dread toward the delivery date. Apart from trying to fool myself into thinking that some gift might come along from the heavens that would allow me to get out of my commitment (laryngitis, lip paralysis, death), I continued to harass the heavens for help.

On the day of the event I still could not envision myself in front of an audience without experiencing the horrors that had haunted me in the theater. The event was to take place outside on a farm, in the late afternoon, and I was to stand on a hay wagon to speak to the group. I was up to my old tricks again, trying to work out how I was going to stand at the entrance of the event greeting the one hundred and some members of my community as they filed in, and just minutes later convince myself that they did not exist. Most of the people expected to attend were friends—which, if you have ever had stage fright, you will understand only worsens the symptoms, as most of us would rather make an ass of ourselves in front of people whom we will never have to see again.

That afternoon, as the cars pulled in for the fundraiser, my courage was running on empty. I stood welcoming our guests as they streamed in, fantasizing that they might suddenly discover that they had to leave before the speeches. "So sorry, left something on the stove!" one of them might say, with the rest following in sympathy.

It wasn't until after I had greeted most of my neighbors that I had a revelation. "Hey, wait a minute," I thought, "These are my friends, my community. I love these people!"

I was coming awake. Instead of shutting the little window of my heart and imagining myself in isolation, why not throw that window open, let the love flood in? Why not allow that love to spill over and embrace every attending soul? I had it all backwards! Why would I mentally run away from my audience, as if I were being chased by them, rather than run toward them, as if coming in for a big group hug? Which move would be more useful to my nerves? And, though I did not voice the thought, for that might have worried my audience, I mentally reached out to all who sat looking up at me, "I love you! All of you! Love you!" What came next was quite miraculous. I was visited by the sweetest sense of calm and went on to deliver my speech with something that almost resembled serenity.

I had uncovered the secret to confident communication, discovered the roots of true courage. A little late, you might be thinking, but I don't think I was meant to remain an actor all of my life. I wanted to be a storyteller, or rather the one who came up with the stories. Furthermore, the lessons that came from suffering stage fright and my eventual awakening to that which would finally conquer my fear are precious to me. I now understand the concept that love has the power to cast out fear. I have felt this on my skin.

Since this discovery, I have taken the method of heart-opening and applied it to many other situations. If, before walking into a room of people whom I don't know, for instance, I remind myself that I love them, even if the fact is not immediately obvious to any of us, it makes a great difference to our conversations. It deepens them, makes something significant out of an exchange that might otherwise have been awkward, or simply mundane.

It might feel a bit silly to inwardly pronounce one's love for someone to whom one has not yet been introduced. Perhaps it could be looked at as a rehearsal for the day when we will be expected to fall hopelessly in love with all the people of the world. Perhaps we are practicing for the opening night performance of the Dawning of Enlightenment.

"Bravo!" the angels will applaud, "Brava!" The heavenly hosts will chant, "Bravissimo!!"

28 🌸

The Eleventh Hour

M Y FAVORITE book of all time is one of Charles Dickens' lesser-known novels, entitled *Dombey and Son*. The story revolves around a cold-hearted businessman and his two children, a son and a daughter. The former is adored by Mr. Dombey and the latter is painfully neglected. The children's mother, the only person to whom the daughter Florence might have looked for love, dies just hours after giving birth to the son, and the father, desperate and unable to express his feelings, bestows all of the love from his stingy heart on his newborn son and turns his back completely on his daughter. Florence, much wounded, somehow manages to keep alive the hope that her father might need her at some point, and she will have the opportunity to express her love for him. She is the picture of unconditional love, though at a certain point in the story she is forced to leave her father's house entirely. The book is nine-hundred pages long, and somewhere around page eight hundred eighty-eight Mr. Dickens brings this proud and cold man to his knees. It seems that even Mr. Dombey has blood coursing through his veins, though through much of the novel the reader will consider him hopelessly inflexible, and incapable of change.

I have a friend who tells me that her father, a difficult and rigid man, tells her that he doesn't approve of end-of-life awakenings, death-bed conversions. *Dombey and Son* would not be the book for this man. The mean should die mean, he believes, and be forced to pay for their meanness. I presume he is envisioning a scenario involving some version of eternal roasting, complete with red devils and pitchforks.

I love a good awakening story, no matter how late in life it occurs. If we are eternal, as those who buy into the concept of hell believe, then our lives could be likened to a paragraph inside a Dickens novel. Whenever enlightenment occurs, it is a welcome guest.

This said, I will often lose sight of the promise of awakening when I meet a particularly recalcitrant personality. "That cake is baked, I'm afraid," I have been known to say when discussing a raging blowhard, angry bigot, dictator, miser, bully.

My husband and I once dined on the side patio of a little restaurant in the Bahamas. At one point we turned to see a door that we guessed led into the bar. The door was closed, and on it hung a sign that read: Door Closed. We took a picture of it. The door, you understand, had to be closed in order for the sign to be read. And the sign, nailed onto the back of this closed door read: Door Closed.

Some people exhibit this sort of redundancy. They are not only closed, but they like to tell you how closed they are. I presume they do this in an attempt to convince you to leave them alone. It often works.

But here is something that I have discovered: if we focus, as is very tempting, on the unenlightened part of the difficult personality, if we stare at the Door Closed sign, we trap him or her with our thoughts in the very behavior that has shut the door to the hope of change.

Charles Dickens never allows for hope to die entirely. There is always a character in his novels that holds to the idea that a person can change, a character that represents the heart of unconditional love. If we look carefully, we might discover that there are people who have played this role for us in our lives, those who have believed in our goodness, in our capability to live good lives. Some of these will play major roles, a grandparent for instance, and some minor roles. These are the ones who will cheer for our better selves to win the race against our less developed selves, and who stand prepared for our eventual awakening, even if it does not arrive until the eleventh hour.

Novelists have employed this device since they picked up the quill. All will look as if it is lost, all hope buried, until the story's conclusion, when lovers finally confess their love, justice is finally served, monsters are finally redeemed.

I am reminded of the time I spent in the theater, both as a young actress in a small repertory theater troupe in New York City and later as a playwright. Near the end of every rehearsal period there would come a moment when everyone involved in the production would be convinced that the show was in such a state of chaos that we simply could not open without public humiliation. As we were sewing ourselves in our costumes during the five minutes before the curtain rose, I fantasized about one of us walking out on stage and sheepishly apologizing to the audience, "We must ask your forgiveness for bringing you here tonight. We have done so under the false pretense that we were prepared to do justice to this play. Please forgive our hubris and return to your homes."

But interestingly, we always managed to rise to the occasion. Actors who had never known their lines during rehearsal delivered them in perfect order—or near enough—lights lit us, sound arrived on cue, costumes did not drop around our ankles. It was always the same and each time it seemed to us an eleventh-hour miracle that the show had been pulled off without disaster.

The artistic director of our little repertory company was a troubled woman who struggled with alcoholism. I overheard two young women in the company one day discussing whether or not this woman was ever likely to recover. "No, never," said one of them, "she is a hopeless addict."

"Never say never," the other one argued, "She might have some sort of reckoning. Her story isn't over yet."

At the time I didn't know which opinion to accept. I wish I could say that it was the one that offered hope. I now understand that I would have been siding with the great author in the sky, the one who never gives up on us.

Perhaps twenty years later, I heard that our artistic director had died. But, before she left the world, five years before, she managed, with the help of Alcoholics Anonymous, to stop drinking.

I wonder how much the attitude of the young member who had held out hope for her had played in her recovery. Perhaps it tipped the delicate scale? I'd like to think it did.

29

Spend Some Love

WHEN YOU love a house, you hope that the next owners will love it at least as much as you do. The idea of selling a beloved house to someone only interested in its resale value would be disheartening, to say the least. Not only would it be an insult to your love of the place, but such a waste for the buyers who can only think of what it will bring them when they sell. One is tempted to ask, "But how long do you intend to put off loving?" Surely life on the planet is temporary enough. Best to find somewhere to live that you can love while you are here. It will ease any home-sickness you might have for the spiritual world. Better yet, find and make a home that you hope resembles your ideal, eternal home (a preview of coming attractions), and bring a little heaven into your earthly existence. I do not imply spending all of your means on your home, just some of your love.

I have loved my house for over thirty years now, and the love has only increased as I fill it more and more with things that I love: paintings by people whom I love, animals that I cannot help but love, plants that depend on my loving them, house guests and dinner guests whom I love.

We used to have some ghostly activity in our 200-year-old home. Whenever we rearranged the furniture in the room where I write, things would be mysteriously upset in a corner of the room. When we went away from the house and returned, we would discover photos knocked over, books pushed around. One night we heard a large crash downstairs, ran down and into this room where these disturbances typically took place, and in the corner, we found a large wind chime on the floor. Nothing was wrong with the hook on which it hung, or the wind chime itself. Our only conclusion was that it had been lifted up off of its hook, that was firmly screwed into the ceiling, and dropped to the floor. We simply picked it up and hung it again.

After that night, Matt suggested that we put things that we loved in the corner of this room. We collected some of our favorite items: a glass etching of a tree, a cross made of red stained glass, a small porcelain deer, and a wooden icon of Saint Francis. We have never had another episode of ghostly commotion since. It sounds a bit counterintuitive to offer things up that one loves to be possibly tossed around and broken, but love can be mysteriously persuasive.

Many of us postpone love in some way or another, waiting for it to arrive in the perfect, preconceived package: the financially solvent husband, the ideal, motherly wife, the picture-perfect home. I knew a woman who lived in the projects in Harlem for many years. One day she decided to paint murals along the walls on the hall outside of the apartment where she lived with her family. She painted animals and cartoon characters for the children. All of the kids in the building wanted to move to her floor. This woman was to eventually move with her family to Wisconsin and into a roomier, safer home, but not before she had spent some of her love on the place where she lived.

You can sense a house come to life when it is loved, not by decorating—walk into any sample room, demonstration home, and if you are like me, you will feel a bit chilled—but by a human expending loving attention.

Of course, there are many other ways to spend love

other than on one's home. And lately, I have been practicing an exercise upon waking first thing in the morning. I attempt to locate from the previous day times in which I felt an outflowing of love. These could be very small—a moment with one of my dogs, a word between friends. After identifying and expressing gratitude for these gifts, I ask the heavens to help me to find more such opportunities during the day before me. "Please show me where I might spend some love today," I suggest.

Sometimes in my woods in the morning I will send an animal a blast of love. I swear the little creatures feel it. I cannot hug a chipmunk, for instance, but when I see one along my walk and tell him that I love him, the little thing appears to scamper around and sing with more gusto than usual. Sometimes—this is, I admit, a tad odd—on first coming upon a body of water: a river, lake, ocean, I will be moved to greet it with a loud, "Well, hello!" as if surprised by the sudden appearance of a dear old friend. My grandmother would have said that perhaps the body of water possesses a water spirit that is visible to my inner sight. Perhaps this is true. It does feel a genuine response to someone, some being.

My yellow Labrador, Cotton, is innately shy around displays of love. Hesitant to look us in the eyes when we tell her we love her, she will loudly yawn. If we suggest that she come to us for a hug, she will back up slightly, not quite sure what to do. Suspecting that Cotton is simply timid and would probably thoroughly enjoy a hug if it were forced upon her, we practice daily enforced huggy-time. We bend over her and wrap her in a firm embrace, and at the same time feel the movement of her torso as her tail wags happily back and forth. My other dogs have all insisted on this daily pleasure, but Cotton prefers it to arrive as a surprise attack. Like a child with autism, she seems to shun such attention, but she clearly delights to feel herself inside a pair of strong, loving arms.

Sometimes we don't know how much we need love until it is offered. "I'm a recluse," you might hear someone say, "I don't need people." "Baloney," I often think to myself, "Just you wait. One day love will catch up to you and hug the solitary right out of you. Your tail won't stop wagging."

We spend money, we spend time, we spend effort, but also waste time, waste money, waste effort. Love is never wasted. One might argue with this reasoning. "I wasted a lot of love on that relationship." But love does not work on a quid pro quo basis. While you are loving, you are benefitting from the process, whether the one you love is loving you back or not. One of the laws of love is that it always feeds the one who loves. This is the sort of spending where it is always right to be extravagant. Love, I emphasize, not longsuffering. One can both love and set healthy boundaries.

Hopefully, at the end of our lives, having lavished the world with love, our pockets will be empty. "Oh dear," we will say, rummaging around in side pockets, patting chest pockets, "not a single coin left." "Mmmm," we will conclude as we begin to float heavenward, "Must be time to head home."

30

The Gifts of Aging

WHEN I was a kid, I spent almost every daylight hour outside during the summer. I ran and played and biked and horsed around, sometimes on horses. At some point during the season my stepfather's ancient mother would come for a visit. In her mid-nineties at the time, she was perfectly delightful, but decidedly inert, and if one wished to enjoy her company it required a willingness to be as immobile as she.

As I dashed around and cavorted with my dash-around pals, I would occasionally sprint past my stepfather and his mother sitting on a bench contemplating some small patch of garden. "Whoa," I would think to myself, "I will never be able to slow down long enough to watch a bunch of flowers grow. I would go mad!"

I have always found it a chore to slow down long enough to visit with someone during daylight hours while sitting on my rear end. Most of the time, when I want to have a nice talk with a friend, I will ask them to take a walk with me, something my sister calls a walkie-talkie. There is a lovely path in my area that runs along the Delaware River Canal where two people can walk side-by-side. An alternative route is the narrow path in the nearby park where I take my morning walks, but it forces one to walk with one's friend as a couple of cows might, staring at the other's tail in single file. Most often my friends and I will opt for the canal path. There is much to be said for stirring the mind with movement while talking things out with a friend. The exercise has produced many "ah-ha" moments, with solutions arrived at, knotty issues straightened out, questions answered. I am very grateful for this continued practice, but I understand that I may not always have the luxury of this custom, given that my joints are exhibiting the signs of rust, and several of my peers are now unable to join me. This has me thinking that it may be valuable to learn to visit with a friend while seated. In fact, this might be one of those gifts of aging that you hear of, a skill that I will be happy to have learned. I suspect it will come with some sweet rewards.

My husband will tell you that I have always wanted to be an old person, but not necessarily an ancient person. I was often happiest hanging out with my mother's middle-aged pals, they seemed to have arrived somewhere I wanted to be. Age levels the playing field, it is the great equalizer, even though it will look quite different on each of us.

When we are young, we think it important to find a way to stand out, to separate ourselves from the human pool of talent, courage, strength, power. We are caught up in the effort to rise above the crowd. This effort might go on for decades before we are willing to let go of the struggle. If we are fortunate, at some point in our later years, we will understand that whatever achievement we were able to attain in our professions, in our communities, it is very likely that our true life's work has been the shaping of our character. "Who did you become?" might be the initial words out of St. Peter's mouth upon your arrival at the pearly gates, and not "Wow, look what you accomplished!"

You might be thinking, but what of the great inventors, great statesmen, what of the timeless books of great writers? What of our legacies?

I have benefitted greatly from certain authors and am truly grateful for their willingness to sit in a quiet room and write and write for hours upon hours—on their seats, I presume—and for their willingness to persevere against all odds to have their writings published. Who would I have become without George MacDonald or Ralph Waldo Emerson? I have also undoubtedly profited from inventions as well, electricity, for instance, and should perhaps give credit to Thomas Edison whenever I turn a lamp switch, or the Ford family whenever I hop in my car, but my sense is that these ideas would have eventually found their way through some channel or other.

The conduit: the writer, inventor, composer, mathematician is simply that, a conduit for the ideas, ideas that I believe have their origins in the heavens. The human instruments through which the ideas arrive are to be commended, certainly, mainly for their belief in the idea, through thick and mostly thin, but to imagine that these people stand apart from the brotherhood of man is a mistake. To treat someone differently because you view him or her as a genius isn't healthy for either of you. It's typically toward the end of a life, or even after a person has gone to their reward, that the details of the human being behind the presumed genius surface, and it isn't always such a flattering reveal. Take the writer and television darling, Charles Kuralt, who charmed audiences with his *On the Road* segments on CBS for a quarter of a century. Two years after his death it was discovered that Mr. Kuralt had a second shadow family in Montana, unknown to his East Coast family, a fact that was revealed by his will in which he bequeathed his house in Montana to the woman who had shared the house with him for thirty years. It puts things in perspective.

I have come to appreciate the funeral. It seems there are two sorts: those where we are told of the deceased's worldly achievements and those where we learn of their true character. I much prefer the latter. I'm not interested in the person's resume. I want to know who the soul was that I have come to mourn or celebrate. What effect did this spirit have on those closest to it? How did this person touch those with whom they came in contact? These are the questions that interest me.

When Matt and I moved away from New York City, to the rural neighborhoods of Bucks County Pennsylvania, I was delighted by the easy introductions at neighbors' houses. When I got home, I would say to Matt, "That was so nice. No one asked me what I did!" We were able to get to know one another based on our spirits and not our bios. In New York, in the fields that Matt and I were in (music and theater), introductions were too often expressed in terms of career moves and lists of successes. I found this keenly boring.

One of the gifts that comes with the slow pace of increased years is that we are more interested in who the person is than what he or she does, or did, if retired. We can begin to know a person from a level closer to their true selves, we move in toward the heart, where the real treasure is.

When we are through inventing, creating, designing, we are free to be utterly ourselves, no longer wishing to stand apart from the crowd, but rather hoping to feel our connection with the great human family. Our differences now mean much less than our similarities, for we are experiencing, or will experience, many of the same issues as our aging neighbors, and are called upon to offer our empathy. This is often when our true work begins, the job of helping one another through the challenges of our later years. This is when we learn the beautiful lesson of dependence.

31 ❋

Light Work

I BUMPED INTO someone with a familiar face at our local municipal building in the fall of 2020. Well, to be perfectly clear, I bumped into someone whose top half of the head was familiar to me, the half not covered by a mask. And, once I added the top half to the rest, the part extending down from the bottom of the mask, I had just enough information to signal familiarity. But, given this limited information, I could not immediately place this woman (for this was a female) among the constellation of people I know from the hood. I use the term hood here to pretend that my neighborhood is diverse enough to warrant this hip term. It is a fantasy of mine. I believe if I can envision being surrounded by all of the colors and shapes of the global human family, that my neighborhood will some-day manifest this diversity and be a garden of colorful ethnicity. Sigh.

But, back to this semi-familiar woman. She turned to greet me by name. "Hi, Margaret," she said, the top half of her head, that is to say, her eyes, looking happy enough to see me. Now, I was truly in a bind. The only civilized response was to answer her back with a greater degree of exuberance than her own greeting in hopes of masking the deficit of not knowing who she was with a smokescreen of enthusiasm. "Hello! How are you?!!!" I screeched through my mask, waving my hands around like cheerful pom-poms.

And then it hit me. "Oh yes, I know who this is." I said to myself, palms circling, eyes shining, "this is the person who nearly ripped my head off over the phone two years ago, accusing me of being cruel to a friend of hers. And here I am waving at her as if we were long-lost friends."

She had, I have to admit, written me a note of apol-ogy and we had seen each other since that time. But, I am cautious around people who have been that snarly to me. Like a questionable dog, I give them a good bit of distance. I love dogs, as I love people, but once they have shown me their teeth, I will conclude that it is safer to love them from the other side of the fence.

"Well, that's torn it!" I thought to myself. I speak of the veil of protective distance I had been maintaining. "Time to make nice with the volatile one."

Might this be one of those hidden blessings of the pandemic?

Interestingly, I received an email within a week of this occurrence from another volatile one, again, one I had been giving a wide berth, and for a second time decided to let my guard down. I begin to suspect that there is a lesson in all this.

The possibilities of tidying our souls are seemingly endless. We could think of it as cobwebbing. Once a year the barn where my horse lives is cobwebbed. This is executed with brooms and occurs at the end of the spider season. The corners and ceilings of the barn enjoy a thorough sweeping, breaking up the dusty old webs that have added that Halloween creepiness to the corners of the stalls. These are not occupied webs, they are the abandoned ones, last season's webs, full of last season's memories. I can imagine that we have such webs in our souls. It's tempting to ignore them, but if one does this, the hidden corners of the soul tend to get more ghoulish. Perhaps it's best to pull out the broom, and have at it.

I have been reading a book about Padre Pio, the Catholic Priest of San Giovanni Rotondo in southern Italy, who was the parish priest there from the year 1916 to his death in 1968. Beatified by the Church in 1999, Padre Pio is believed to have performed numerous miracles, was known to bilocate, appearing in several places at once, and at times grew so ecstatic that he was said to have lifted off the ground in ecstatic moods. Many books have been written about this marvelous man but the book that I am reading, *Padre Pio and I*, by Adolfo Affatato, is particularly special because it is written from the perspective of one of the Padre's "spiritual sons," a young man whom Padre Pio promised to keep in his special prayers. Adolfo is occasionally given the privilege to visit the Padre during his endless prayer sessions, occasionally asking questions of him. One day he asked the Padre whether he had ever seen God, or as he put it, "have you ever seen Jesus?" The Padre thought for a moment and replied, "God is light. The more a soul is pure, the more it feels the splendor of that light."

This got me thinking about my cobwebs. My suspicion is that if there is anyone in my past, anyone in my present, anyone who is a victim of my scrutiny and, more important, my criticism, is essentially caught up in one of my cobwebs. The sooner I take the broom out and break the old dusty thing up, the closer I will come to being able to experience that splendor of the light to which Padre Pio refers. What am I waiting for?

Periodically, I will mentally sweep out my house. I do this as I lay in bed at night, before I drop off to sleep.

"Ok," I will say to myself, "I think it's time for a good cleaning."

I will then enlist those from the angelic kingdom to help me, inviting in a crew of angels to bring their heavenly brooms and meet me on the top floor of my house. We have an attic that was renovated to hold two small bedrooms. I picture myself standing in one of these rooms and waiting for my heavenly crew. When they are gathered, we all pick up our brooms and begin to sweep. We sweep and sweep and sweep, kicking up the dust, attacking every corner. At some point we head down the stairs at a gallop, brushing everything before us: all of the unwanted feelings, crusty thoughts, misunderstandings, hurts, stupidities. We hustle them down the stairs and go to work on the second floor, dashing around, flying up into corners, sweeping out every hidey-hole, and then tumble down to the bottom floor, all the while working with a fierce enthusiasm. We scour the bottom floor, brooms flying, gathering, gathering, and then open the front door and swing our brooms wildly out the door, brushing everything, every single particle of negativity out into the night.

"Out!" we cry, "Out with you and don't come back," after which I hastily shut the door, throw my back against it and take in our clean and sparkling house. Sweet.

The final step is to ask my heavenly hosts to place a dome of protection over the house, something I imagine to be porous, made of a substance like gossamer and stitched together with the principle of light.

"Only light can enter here," I announce to my surroundings. "Only good."

32 ✿

Slow Prayers

I MUST ASSUME that most of us have said prayers for which no answer seems to arrive, prayers that appear to be way past their expiration date. These are the prayers where we lose sight of how long it has been since we started praying them. Was it three days, three years, three decades ago? Like a neglected customer at a crowded diner, we wonder, "Hey, what's it take to get some service around here?"

I've prayed such prayers over the years. I had a ten-year-long prayer to find a way of reaching an audience for my thoughts on faith before I stumbled upon the idea of Listen Well. When no answer seems to arrive for a long-held prayer, I can grow doubtful of my prayer methods: "What am I doing wrong here?" C.S. Lewis wrote that he believed the body should be in a position of prayer as well as the mind. "Should I be on my knees?" I wonder. "Should I whisper? Shout? Spin like a Whirling Dervish?"

Maybe some prayers are just slow. You've heard of Slow Food. Why not Slow Prayers?

I have launched prayer campaigns that have stretched out over many decades. Mainly I pray for help, for a solution to present itself. And I try and make myself available to help toward the prayer's resolution. My prayers are delivered to God, I assume, but when He doesn't appear to be listening, I look around for someone who might have his ear. Jesus is of course one of those who presumably has an inside seat, but there are other obvious insiders. Angels are high on the call list. The other day, while worrying over a long-held prayer, I wondered whether I might enlist the help of the Blessed Mother. I am not a Catholic and have never learned to pray the rosary, but I did once appeal to Mary when I was worried sick about an actress in my play who was having difficulties.

This was five years ago when I had gathered some of my old theater pals to do some development work on a play. We were set to perform the piece for three nights to see how it worked with an audience. We had enjoyed a wonderful, creative rehearsal period. The four actors, all in their sixties, were beautifully suited to their roles. The problem was that after a certain age, it can be a challenge to learn lines. One of our cast members was struggling more than the others with this issue, and I was beginning to seriously doubt whether we were going to be able to go through with the planned weekend of performances. Our crew had managed in only a week to turn a friend's barn into an intimate theater. Everything looked in order on the morning of the first public performance: the barn was magically transformed with lights, sound system, raked seating for over a hundred audience members, and yet there remained this niggling issue: our actress, though glorious in her part, appeared unable to get through a scene without stopping and asking for her lines.

On the morning of the first night's performance, we had an early, difficult rehearsal and broke for lunch. I had a brief conversation with the director, where we pondered whether or not to have a script available onstage in case of a complete derailment. We came to no conclusion and the cast and crew went off to find something to eat. I chose to stay behind. My first thought was to sweep the barn, and as I did so, to pray. I have always found sweeping therapeutic, and if I accompany this activity with prayer, the combination can feel quite powerful. I swept and prayed and thought about all of the happy events that had taken place in that barn.

My friend Jill, who owns the barn, had been gathering friends over the years for parties and fundraisers here. She would often punctuate the evening's fun with parades of her giraffe-sized, hand-crafted puppets: animal puppets, vegetable puppets, some crazy-looking skeletons for the Day of the Dead celebration.

At some point after much sweeping and begging, I thought perhaps I would go to the upper level of the barn and visit some of Jill's puppets. I am not sure why I chose to do this. Perhaps, feeling as desperate as I was, I thought it prudent to fill every corner of the barn with prayer. When I arrived upstairs all was in darkness apart from one stark light bulb shining on a small door against a back wall. On this door hung a woven blanket in warm desert colors: browns and yellows. It was purchased, I was to learn later, in New Mexico. The image on the blanket was of a young Virgin Mary. The single light revealed her gentle figure, tender expression. I no longer had any interest in the lifeless puppets around me, all of my attention was on Mary.

"Oh, I have never thought to ask for your help," I began, "and I know this is not such a large issue in the great scheme of things, but could you bless this evening's performance? Could you help our good friend to remember her lines?" I said no more, feeling that my petition was clear, and stayed with her for a few more minutes before stepping carefully around the piles of puppets and moving back down the stairs.

That evening's performance was a miracle. I do not know how my actress friend went from constantly asking for help with her lines to delivering such a perfectly confident, charming performance. It ended up being one of those rare, magical evenings in the theater when the relationship between audience and performers seemed electric. I was overwhelmed with gratitude.

I have read many accounts of Marian appearances: in Lourdes, Fatima, Guadalupe, Medjugorje, to name just a few. A friend's mother had been miraculously cured of cancer by visiting Medjugorje, Herzegovina. In my study of these documented visitations I have been impressed (or perhaps I should be more honest and confess, slightly disappointed) by the simplicity of the message that Mary has delivered. This advice is essentially to pray and to turn away from hatred and toward love—though in Fatima, apparently, she put on some fancy fireworks for the crowds with the sun in full spin and other marvels—but again, her message is the same:

pray and dispel hatred. Replace hatred with love. Love, she suggests, holds the power to change the direction of events. Love can avert war and heal a broken world. One person loving another could be the tipping point to peace. Why did I find this message lacking when I was younger? Did I expect the Virgin Mary to appear and tell us who we were to vote for in the next election? To argue the merits of socialism over capitalism? I hope I have matured enough to understand her meaning.

My thinking today is that Mary's message is the only piece of advice she could have delivered. The cure for the world's ills is in everyone's hands. It is so very simple. So simple that even a child, or perhaps I should say, only the child spirit in each of us, could fully grasp it. It's so simple and yet worth all of our prayers, slow or otherwise. "Help us. Please help us to love more."

33

Labor of Love

I STOPPED TO speak to a man the other day, the owner of a farm for retired horses where I was keeping my horse. He was on a mower at the time and turned off the engine to chat. I commented on how beautiful his farm was, adding that my old mare enjoyed a better view than I did. "It's a labor of love," he told me in reference to his farm.

I thought, but did not say, "Oh lucky you for having one of those!"

The expression "a labor of love" has always implied a pejorative. In other words, this effort will never make me any money, will never further my career, but I love it and care for it out of that love. There are some people, sadly, who have never allowed themselves to indulge in such a labor.

I imagine these opportunities for loving are offered to us regularly and perhaps as often refused. But Love is awfully persuasive and will likely have its way with us in the end.

"Never hire a friend," an old boss will warn, and then proceed to fall head-over-heels in friendship with a new employee. There are all sorts of ways in which a relationship will burgeon into love. Sometimes a person in one's life will grow ill and become dependent, cracking the crust off the heart of the one on which they are dependent. Pets will often have the effect of scraping away any resistance to love on the part of their owners. A pet is never completely independent and therefore their care is always an invitation to a labor of love. Lucky the laborer, I say.

In my late forties, I took on the ownership of a horse. I did not intend to do so and was fiercely warned by the voices of doubt inside my head not to be so foolhardy, but I persevered. I fell in love with her. And then one day she was very badly injured. I fell more deeply in love. The more she needed me the more I loved. My love for her changed my life, so much so that I wrote a book about her, about us, and the ways in which love changed both of our lives. I titled the book *The Parables of Sunlight* because this period of intense loving seemed to carry a number of equally intense, daily teachings, filled with new understanding. Pardon the book plug, I do this to illustrate the conniving manipulations of Love.

We are never safe from love. It seems we're a population of suckers, sitting ducks, each one of us. Love could come crashing through our hearts at any moment. Pow.

When a labor of love is being presented to me, I will often feel something that I would describe as a call to task. Even if inspired to make a phone call, I will feel the nudge to action. And I would estimate that half the time I disregard the prompting or shelve it for later. I am not proud of this ratio and am trying to be more mindful, hoping to learn to act on these divine urges without delay.

My suspicion is that if we can be trained to respond to the slightest inspiration, say to speak to someone next to us on a train, or write an email, or pick up the phone, we might be prepared in the future to take on a more daunting task, say to leap into a difficult situation to save someone.

When my mother was in the mid-stages of Alzheimer's disease, the family hired a nurse to oversee her care. Her name was Vera and she and my mother fell instantly into deep friendship. Though other nurses came in to spell Vera, no other nurse had quite the same effect on Mom as did Vera. This love between them was perfectly mutual. Although Vera had never known my mother in her healthy, younger mind, she knew her essence and loved her. After my mother died, Vera separated from her husband and moved into an apartment. She told me later that she had taken with her only one framed photo to put into her new home, and this was a picture of my mother. Sometimes our labors of love will arrive inside our career callings.

Looking back on our lives, could we ever have imagined the company of souls that we came here to love? This choir of spirits is often filled with the strangest assortment of characters (human and animal) that have managed to push their ways into our hearts.

I believe that we came here to love, simply to love; that incarnation on Earth is a sort of call to task, and that task is to love. I used to wonder when I was younger, what sort of lessons I was to learn on Earth, as if I had misbehaved in a previous school of life and had to repeat a grade. I no longer believe that I was born to enter the school of hard knocks in order to improve myself. Indeed, much of what I have learned has indicated that I had more to unlearn than learn, that a lifetime's pile-up of restrictive thinking was the very thing of which I needed to rid myself. The more I have managed to let go of the concept of life being an academy of humiliations and embrace my mistakes, accept myself with all my failings and disappointments, the more the windows and doors of my soul have opened to love.

The Sufi poet Rumi writes, "Out beyond ideas of wrongdoing and right doing, there is a field. I'll meet you there..."

I had a dream recently that seemed to support the idea of love being the purpose of life. I have had many dreams in the past several years where I am attempting to find a new place to live. I understand that I was perfectly content with my last house, and lament the choice to move, but the decision has already been made, and I find myself looking at possible homes in which to live. In a recent dream, I am standing outside a house, lamenting the departure of my old familiar home, and wondering how I could possibly make this new house feel as if it were mine. I turn to see a man approaching. I know him and very much admire him. I understand he is streets beyond me on the path of enlightenment and am honored by his presence. I suppose, for this reason, I open up to him about my doubts around this move to a new home. I wonder what I might put in this new house to make it mine. The seller had used it to store his collection of automobiles. I could see the cars through the windows, neatly lined up on the first and second floors.

My companion turns to me and says, "It doesn't matter what you put in the house, Margaret. I only ask that you place your ring in it."

As with most teaching dreams, I snapped instantly awake and began to think about the ideas that were conveyed. The previous owner's collection of cars filling his entire house, even the upstairs bedrooms, seemed to push the limits of what I might consider the proper use of a home. "It doesn't matter what you put in the house…" The house, I understood, represented a life, a journey through life. But what was the significance of the ring, I wondered? A wedding ring, I thought, is a symbol of love and promise. It signifies a commitment to love.

It doesn't matter what you put in your house of existence, whether this is a life in politics or construction, a life filled with canvasses and paints, spreadsheets, herds of cows, treasured cats, supper for eleven for eleven thousand days—what matters is your commitment to love.

This is our labor of love, this life. This is our call to task: to love what we are called to love, here, now. We're all laborers in the fields of Love. The harvest of such labor is love. More and more love.

The end

MARGARET wrote plays for many years before taking up essay writing. In 2010 she launched ListenWell.org, a spoken word website offering once monthly recorded essays exploring divine themes. Her writings can be found, among other places, in Parabola, Thrive Global, Elephant Journal, World Religion News, Read the Spirit, Day One and Big Muddy.

Her books include *To Hear the Forest Sing (a selection of writings from Listen Well)*, and *The Parables of Sunlight (A memoir of a farm)*.

She lives in Bucks County Pennsylvania in an old stone farmhouse with her musician husband Matt Balitsaris. Her spoken word essays can now also be found on your favorite podcast App. Search "Listen Well," and look for the owl.

For more information visit ListenWell.Org

CPSIA information can be obtained
at www.ICGtesting.com
Printed in the USA
BVHW042251110622
639579BV00004B/132